Pra

HIS REDEEM

"David Fisler has given us a compelling picture of the process of repentance. He draws us into the lives of those who seek forgiveness and makes us eager to seek our own change of heart—for are we not all sinners?"

—Virginia H. Pearce, author and former counselor
in the Young Women general presidency

"I highly recommend this excellent book as a fresh, concise, and inspiring guide to how the power of the Atonement and the Lord's grace help us to repent, change, and become new creatures in Christ (see Mosiah 27:26; 2 Corinthians 5:17)."

—Lloyd D. Newell, speaker and
author of *The Gospel of Second Chances*

"David Fisler has written a compelling book to help us become clean and pure. His book *His Redeeming Power: Cleansed on Conditions of Repentance* carefully explains each point of the process of repentance and is a much-needed book for your library. The principle of repentance is explained in detail with the power of the Atonement. It is perfect for the teenager and adult. It inspires us to make the mighty change."

—Ed J. Pinegar, author of *The Temple*; *A Mighty Change*;
Gethsemane, Golgotha, and the Garden Tomb;
and *The Little Book of Gratitude for Latter-day Saints*

"*His Redeeming Power* is an amazing, thought-provoking review of the doctrine of repentance. It is replete with scriptural references and is comprehensive in nature. *His Redeeming Power* is a marvelous reference source for any member, teacher, or leader in the Church who wants to more fully understand the doctrine of repentance and how it relates to the infinite Atonement and the love the Savior has for everyone."

—Kenneth A. Ellsworth, Penasquitos California Stake president

HIS REDEEMING
POWER

Dear Bob and Fern,

I am very grateful for our friendship and for your thoughtful concern for our family!

I thoroughly enjoyed writing this book because I felt the Spirit every time I worked on it.

May the Lord bless you and your family!

Love,
Dave
3/3/16

HIS REDEEMING
POWER

CLEANSED *on* CONDITIONS *of* REPENTANCE

DAVID P. FISLER

CFI
An Imprint of Cedar Fort, Inc.
Springville, Utah

ISBN 13: 978-1-4621-1770-3

Published by CFI, an imprint of Cedar Fort, Inc.
2373 W. 700 S., Springville, UT 84663
Distributed by Cedar Fort, Inc., www.cedarfort.com

Library of Congress Cataloging-in-Publication Data

Names: Fisler, David P., 1958- author.
Title: His redeeming power / David P. Fisler.
Description: Springville, Utah : CFI, An imprint of Cedar Fort, Inc., [2016]
 | 2016 | Includes bibliographical references and index.
Identifiers: LCCN 2015035047 | ISBN 9781462117703 (perfect bound : alk. paper)
Subjects: LCSH: Repentance--Church of Jesus Christ of Latter-day Saints. |
 Church of Jesus Christ of Latter-day Saints--Doctrines. | Mormon
 Church--Doctrines.
Classification: LCC BX8656 .F57 2016 | DDC 234/.5--dc23
LC record available at http://lccn.loc.gov/2015035047

Cover design by Shawnda T. Craig
Cover design © 2016 Cedar Fort, Inc.
Edited and typeset by Jessica B. Ellingson

Printed in the United States of America

10 9 8 7 6 5 4 3 2 1

Printed on acid-free paper

To Joan

CONTENTS

CONTENTS

PREFACE

As a former bishop and now as a branch president, I have met with many members who wanted to repent of their sins and obtain forgiveness from the Lord but didn't know how to do so. Some were unaware of the magnitude of their transgressions, particularly serious sexual sins. To help them better understand the glorious and vital "doctrine of repentance" (D&C 68:25), I desired to give them a small book that explained repentance and its associated gospel principles in short, easy-to-read chapters—both for their personal study and to review in our discussions together. Unable to find such a book, I decided to write one. There are other much more exhaustive books on the subject (such as Spencer W. Kimball's *The Miracle of Forgiveness*) and books containing chapters on repentance, but I hope you will find this concise, dedicated work to be a valuable guide on how to repent and a source of encouragement as you seek forgiveness.

ACKNOWLEDGMENTS

I am grateful to my wife, Joan, for her constant love and support. I appreciate her numerous insightful and candid suggestions that have made this book significantly better. I am thankful to Dale and Carla Greer and Jose and Brenda Noel for their careful and meticulous review of the manuscript and for their many ideas and comments that have also greatly improved this work. Notwithstanding the wonderful assistance I have received, I am, of course, solely responsible for any errors contained herein.

A NOTE ON QUOTES

To protect the identity of those whom I have loved and served, some quotes used in this book that reference a particular sin, while correctly capturing the member's feelings and emotions, have been altered, and the sin or circumstances spoken of have been generalized or changed. Some names, where appropriate, have also been changed.

INTRODUCTION

His Redeeming Power is a doctrinally based guidebook on how to repent. While it also covers why we need to repent, it does not, with a few exceptions, discuss specific sins or ways to avoid sin.

The Savior has commanded each of us to "search the scriptures" (John 5:39). Samuel the Lamanite told the Nephites, "The holy scriptures . . . leadeth . . . to faith on the Lord, and unto repentance, which faith and repentance bringeth a change of heart" (Helaman 15:7). The scriptures are the real handbook, the true guide. They will "lead the [followers] of Christ in a strait and narrow course . . . and land their souls, yea, their immortal souls, at the right hand of God in the kingdom of heaven" (Helaman 3:29–30). Given these truths, *His Redeeming Power* purposely contains many scriptural quotations. I invite you to look up the cited verses and to read them in their entirety and in their full context.

I have made four assumptions about you while writing this book. First, you have (or had in the past) a testimony of Jesus Christ—that He lives, that He loves you, and that He brought to pass "the great and eternal plan of redemption" (Alma 34:16) through His infinite Atonement. Second, your testimony led you to be baptized and enter into a covenant with the Lord to keep His commandments. Third, since we "all have sinned" (Romans 5:12), you have broken one or more of the commandments of God and need to repent. And fourth, you want to repent or are considering doing so.

I encourage you, therefore, as you read this book, to take time to ponder the doctrines contained in each chapter and to consider how you can apply them to your life. I also encourage you to write down the promptings and instructions you are given from the Spirit and to follow the counsel you have received.

This book is divided into three sections. Section 1 covers what it means to repent and the blessings of the Atonement. Section 2 discusses sin, its consequences, and why we should repent. And Section 3 contains a chapter on each condition of repentance.

SECTION 1

WHAT IS REPENTANCE?

A MIGHTY CHANGE *of* HEART

REPENTANCE IS A glorious and exalting principle—a positive principle! It is an essential element of "the great plan of happiness" (Alma 42:8).

Satan continually tries to convince us that repentance is a fearful or negative ordeal. But in reality it is sin and all its consequences we should fear. It is being "exposed to the whole law of the demands of justice" (Alma 34:16) that should cause us "to tremble and shake to the center" (D&C 10:56).

Satan also wants us to think that God is ruthless and unforgiving. Don't believe him! God is not our enemy. He is our loving Father in Heaven, and He desires our exaltation. He has given us the gifts of repentance and forgiveness so that we can become "perfect, even as [He] is perfect" (Matthew 5:48).

WHY IS IT THAT MEN MUST REPENT?

After Adam and Eve partook of the forbidden fruit, they were driven out of the Garden of Eden and cut off from the presence of the Lord—no longer to walk and talk face-to-face with God. They had "transgressed the commandment" and "became spiritually dead" (D&C 29:40–41).

Spiritual death—our separation from God as a result of disobedience—is intended by the Lord to be temporary. Accordingly, and sometime after the Fall, God revealed to Adam the plan of salvation and the mission of Jesus Christ. He taught him of faith, repentance, baptism, and the gift of the Holy Ghost (see Moses 6:50–52).

Desiring to better understand these basic principles and ordinances of the gospel, Adam asked the Lord a simple yet profound question: "Why is it that men must repent?" (Moses 6:53). The Lord replied, "All men, everywhere, must repent, or they can in nowise inherit the kingdom of God, for no unclean thing can dwell . . . in his presence" (Moses 6:57).

We, "by the fall of Adam," are also "considered as dead" (Helaman 14:16), for we too are separated from God and subject to the influences of Satan. And despite our determined efforts to obey the commandments, we have succumbed to many of the enticements and temptations of the devil. We "have sinned, and come short of the glory of God" (Romans 3:23). We have become unclean.

Our situation then is desperate. If we are not cleansed of all our sins, we will remain "shut out from the presence of our God" (2 Nephi 9:9) forever. Our spiritual death will become permanent.

Thankfully, we can become clean again and be reunited with our Father in Heaven. Jesus Christ has "power given unto him from the Father to redeem [us] from [our] sins because of repentance" (Helaman 5:11). The Atonement of Jesus Christ, which was "prepared from the foundation of the world" (Mosiah 4:6), will redeem us from our "individual sins *on conditions of repentance*" (D&C 138:19; emphasis added).

THE CONDITIONS OF REPENTANCE

What are the conditions of repentance? In short, they are all that the Lord requires of us to be forgiven—what we need to do and what we need to become.

Below is a quick overview of the conditions we will examine in detail in individual chapters of this book.[1]

ELIMINATING PRIDE: Pride puts us in opposition to God and is the root of all sin. As we develop humility, we can recognize our transgressions, let go of the excuses that keep us from repenting, and comply with all that the Lord requires of us to be forgiven.

EXERCISING FAITH: We can conquer our sins by increasing our faith in the Lord Jesus Christ. We cannot repent without faith.

GAINING AWARENESS: We acknowledge all our transgressions and take full responsibility for them. To help us recognize our sins, the Lord calls us to repentance in many different ways. For example, He calls to us through the Light of Christ, by the Holy Ghost, and through divine chastening.

Offering prayer: Through prayer we confess our sins to our Father in Heaven, seek His guidance in overcoming our sins, and ask His forgiveness.

Feeling sorrow: We feel godly sorrow for breaking the commandments, and we are anxious to be clean again.

Making confession: We fully disclose our sins to God, to those we have wronged, and, if necessary, to our bishop.

Providing restitution: We do all we can to repair the physical and emotional damage caused by our sins.

Demonstrating obedience: We forever abandon our transgressions and our desires to commit sin. The passage of time without repeating our wrongdoing demonstrates our commitment to be obedient.

Renewing covenants: We renew our covenant to faithfully live all the commandments. We do not ignore some commandments while repenting of others.

Extending forgiveness: We completely and unconditionally forgive others their trespasses against us.

Seeking forgiveness: We plead with Heavenly Father to forgive us of our sins through the Atonement of Jesus Christ.

Repentance is an individual process that varies from person to person and from sin to sin. While all the conditions of repentance apply to most of us most of the time, they too can vary according to our particular sins or to our individual circumstances. We learn the conditions of our repentance by reading the scriptures, receiving personal revelation, and, when appropriate, talking with our bishop.

Although there is an implied order to the conditions listed above (for example, we must recognize our transgressions before we can feel sorrow for them), many overlap each other, and we will undoubtedly be working on several conditions simultaneously.

WHAT DOES IT MEAN TO REPENT?

The scriptures frequently combine the word *repent* with one of the conditions of repentance. Consider the following scriptural verse fragments:

Repent, and harden not your hearts. (Alma 12:33)

Repent and believe. (2 Nephi 30:2)

Sorrowing was not unto repentance. (Mormon 2:13)

Repenting and confessing their sins. (Helaman 16:5)

Repent . . . and restore. (D&C 98:47)

Repent of your sins and forsake them. (Mosiah 4:10)

Repent, and keep the commandments. (D&C 19:13)

Repented and sought forgiveness. (Moroni 6:8)

To repent must therefore mean something more than to comply with an individual condition. Theodore M. Burton, while a member of First Quorum of the Seventy, explained that repentance is more than fulfilling all the conditions of repentance:

> As a General Authority, I have prepared information for the First Presidency to use in considering applications to readmit repentant transgressors into the Church and to restore priesthood and temple blessings. Many times a bishop will write, "I feel he has suffered enough!" But suffering is not repentance. Suffering comes from *lack* of complete repentance. A stake president will write, "I feel he has been punished enough!" But punishment is not repentance. Punishment *follows* disobedience and *precedes* repentance. A husband will write, "My wife has confessed everything!" But confession is not repentance. Confession is an admission of guilt that occurs as repentance begins. A wife will write, "My husband is filled with remorse!" But remorse is not repentance. Remorse and sorrow continue because a person has *not* yet fully repented. Suffering, punishment, confession, remorse, and sorrow may sometimes accompany repentance, but they are not repentance. What, then, *is* repentance?[2]

Indeed, what does it mean to repent if it does not mean to fulfill all the conditions of our repentance? The Lord taught Alma the Younger, "All mankind . . . must be born again; yea, born of God, changed from their carnal and fallen state, to a state of righteousness" (Mosiah 27:25). Repentance means change—to completely change our thoughts, our actions, and our desires from evil to good. Repentance means to have "a mighty change in us, or in our hearts, that we have no more disposition to do evil, but to do good continually" (Mosiah 5:2). We change not only our actions but also the motivation for our actions. We change from being "carnally-minded" to "spiritually-minded" (2 Nephi 9:39).

Alexander Pope, an English poet, observed:

> *Vice is a monster of so frightful mien,*
> *As, to be hated, needs but to be seen;*
> *But seen too oft, familiar with her face,*
> *We first endure, then pity, then embrace.*[3]

True repentance reverses this direction. We move from embracing sin to abhorring it. We arrive at the point where we "shake at the appearance of sin" (2 Nephi 4:31) and have "an everlasting hatred against sin and iniquity" (Alma 37:32; see also Alma 13:12). Repentance, then, is also becoming. It is a continual process, not a one-time event.

As we continue to repent of all our sins and diligently strive to be "true followers" of Jesus Christ, we are "filled with [perfect] love" and "become the [children] of God; that when he shall appear we shall be like him" (Moroni 7:48). To repent is to become more like God.

We have truly repented of our sins when we have fulfilled all the conditions of our repentance and experienced a "mighty change in [our] hearts" (Alma 5:14). In fact, a mighty change of heart is the condition of repentance upon which all others rest.

NOTES

1. Other conditions that may apply to us while we are repenting, such as fasting, sharing the gospel, and studying the scriptures, are discussed in the chapters in Section 3.

2. Theodore M. Burton, "The Meaning of Repentance," *Ensign*, August 1988, 7; emphasis in original.
3. Alexander Pope, *An Essay on Man. In Epistles to a Friend. Epistle II* (London: Printed for J. Wilford, 1733), 217–20; emphasis removed, spelling and capitalization modernized.

The POWER *of* HIS REDEMPTION

*T*O ILLUSTRATE THE beautiful change and joy that comes to those who have repented "with full purpose of heart" (3 Nephi 10:6), let me share, from a bishop's perspective, the process of repentance.

I like to meet regularly with those who have confessed their serious sins and desire to repent. The purpose of our visits is to help strengthen their faith, fortify their resolve to keep the commandments, and increase their understanding of the Atonement of Jesus Christ. We also review what they have been reading in the scriptures and their progress in completing the conditions of their repentance. The length of their repentance process depends on them and on the Lord; my role is to help them progress as directed by the Spirit.

Most individuals who have come to me and confessed their sins have been humble and contrite. They felt intense sorrow for their wrongdoing—a blessing that brought them to repentance. Unfortunately, many have also felt discouraged and hopeless. Satan did not stop trying to destroy them after he successfully enticed them to sin. He continued his assault and convinced them they were worthless and unredeemable, unworthy to approach Heavenly Father in prayer, and no longer loved by Him. In great anguish they have told me: "I am broken," "I feel powerless to change," "These have got to be the worst sins you've ever heard," "My sin is so bad that I might as well give up and commit other sins," "I don't know if I'll make it," "I don't think there's any hope for me," "How can I ever be forgiven?" and "I don't know how God can love me!"

In our initial interviews their pain is palpable and real. But when we meet we are "visited by the Spirit of God" (Alma 9:21). The Holy Ghost reawakens within them their hope and faith and restores to them "light and truth" (D&C 93:39)—knowledge and testimony of the simple principles of the gospel that were taken from them by Satan because of their disobedience.

We read together how the Lord encouraged Joseph Smith after he sinned: "Remember, *God is merciful*; therefore, repent of that which thou hast done which is contrary to the commandment which I gave you, and *thou art still chosen*" (D&C 3:10; emphasis added). And they are comforted in knowing God is forgiving, and they begin to believe they can still be redeemed.

We review how the Lord has blessed and watched over them, how He understands "the weakness of man and how to succor them who are tempted" (D&C 62:1). And they realize "the Lord is on [their] side" (Psalm 118:6)—that He loves them and wants their success and happiness.

We discuss specific ways they can overcome their sins and how to avoid future sin. As we do so, their confidence in their ability to keep the commandments is strengthened. If their obedience falters, we work on developing their humility and increasing their faith—the two foundational conditions of repentance.

As they continue to develop a true change of heart, they are able to fully obey all the commandments. They know that through the Atonement of Jesus Christ all their "sorrow and mourning shall flee away" and "everlasting joy and holiness" (2 Nephi 8:11) can be theirs. They know they can repent and be forgiven of all their sins.

Toward the end of their repentance process, I will almost always ask, "Is there anything else the Lord would have you do to receive forgiveness? I don't want to stop meeting with you until you know in your heart you have been forgiven. I want you to know for sure. The Lord will tell you, and He will tell me. I don't want you, for example, to be sitting in a future sacrament meeting and cringe when the speaker talks about obeying the law of chastity [or whatever the applicable commandment is]."

Most at this point are confident that their change of heart is complete. If they are unsure all the conditions of their repentance have been met, I suggest they ask the Lord if they have left anything undone. Many times, however, the only condition they have remaining is to sincerely ask God, perhaps one more time, for forgiveness.

The next time we meet is usually the sweetest of all our meetings. They share with me their sacred, spiritual experiences of the time when the Holy Ghost did "enter into their hearts, and they were filled as if with fire" (Helaman 5:45). They tearfully recall the moment when the Spirit, in "a still voice of perfect mildness," bore an unmistakable witness to their "very soul[s]" (Helaman 5:30) that they were cleansed and forgiven of all their sins. They try to put into words how they were blessed with perfect peace of mind and "filled with that joy which is unspeakable" (Helaman 5:44). They bear witness of the beauty, power, and majesty of the Atonement and reverently express their profound love and gratitude for their Savior. They humbly testify of their new appreciation for the restored truths of the gospel and, in particular, for their love of the commandments.

In our first meeting they would not lift their heads out of shame as they spoke to me; now they look me square in the eye and are full of confidence and joy. They radiate goodness and purity. The world that was dark, dreary, and full of pain is now beautiful and bright—full of hope and life. Anything is possible, and all the blessings that seemed so distant or lost are once again available to them.

I again express my love and gratitude for them. I tell them I will miss meeting with them, for my testimony has been strengthened and my faith increased as I witnessed the power of the Atonement transform and cleanse them. They came unto Christ and partook of "the power of his redemption" (Omni 1:26), and their change was truly miraculous.

THE ATONEMENT OF JESUS CHRIST

Our miraculous change and the Lord's redeeming power qualify us to return to God's presence. Our Father in Heaven knew we would commit sins, even serious ones, as we use our agency to learn good from evil. Yet He doesn't despise us for our wrongdoing, nor does He desire our misery. In fact, "God so loved the world, that he gave his only begotten Son, that whosoever believeth in him should not perish, but have everlasting life" (John 3:16).

Jesus Christ also loves us, and He loves us perfectly and individually. He willingly offered "himself a sacrifice for sin" (2 Nephi 2:7), enduring "exquisite" (D&C 19:15) pain in our behalf. He briefly described His suffering in a revelation given through the Prophet Joseph Smith:

> I, God, have suffered these things for all, that they might not suffer if they would repent; . . . Which suffering caused myself, even God, the greatest of all, to tremble because of pain, and to bleed at every pore, and to suffer both body and spirit. (D&C 19:16, 18)

The Atonement of Jesus Christ rescues each of us from physical death (see 1 Corinthians 15:22) and saves us (except for the sons of perdition) into a kingdom of glory, eternally free from the grasp of Satan (see D&C 76:43). But our Savior wants to do more than deliver us from death and the devil. He wants to wash us clean of sin's scarlet stains (see Isaiah 1:18) and to free us from the terrible punishments demanded by justice; He wants us to be reunited eternally with our Father in Heaven.

Jesus Christ does all He can to lead us to repentance and to help us repent. After our change of heart is complete, we plead with our Father in Heaven to have mercy and to "apply the atoning blood of Christ that we may receive forgiveness of our sins" (Mosiah 4:2). Jesus, who is our "advocate with the Father" (D&C 45:3), also petitions God, saying,

> Father, . . . behold the blood of thy Son which was shed, the blood of him whom thou gavest that thyself might be glorified; Wherefore, Father, spare these my brethren that believe on my name, that they may come unto me and have everlasting life. (D&C 45:4–5)

Our Father in Heaven then forgives us of our sins. He takes "away the guilt from our hearts" (Alma 24:10) and grants us mercy through the sacrifice of His Son. Justice is satisfied, and we are encircled "in the arms of safety" (Alma 34:16). We are worthy again to return to His presence.

Adam, through whom "sin entered into the world" (Romans 5:12), looked forward to the restorative power of the Atonement and jubilantly testified, "Blessed be the name of God, for . . . again in the flesh I shall see God" (Moses 5:10).

SECTION 2

WHY REPENT?

The WHOLE WORLD LIETH *in* SIN

ITH TEAR-STAINED CHEEKS, one sister concluded her heartfelt and moving, even eloquent, confession: "I'm done. I'm done with these sins and with the way I'm living. I'm done degrading myself and letting others pull me down. I'm done being miserable. I know who I am and who I can become. I know my Savior still loves me, and Heavenly Father will still forgive me."

This sweet sister recognized the Savior had never stopped inviting her to repent. In fact, since "the whole world lieth in sin" (D&C 84:49), He continues to invite everyone to repent. He turns no one away. "Come unto me all ye ends of the earth," He beckons, "buy milk and honey, without money and without price" (2 Nephi 26:25). His "arm is lengthened out all the day long" (2 Nephi 28:32), and "his hand is stretched out still" (Isaiah 5:25).

THE THING OF MOST WORTH

The Lord, knowing the eternal consequences of sin, tells His servants, "The thing which will be of the most worth unto you will be to declare repentance unto this people" (D&C 15:6; see also D&C 16:6). In fact, He commands them, stating, "Say nothing but repentance unto this generation" (D&C 6:9). As members of the Church, we too are obligated to "invite all to come unto Christ" (D&C 20:59).

In my responsibility to persuade members to repent (see 2 Nephi 26:27), several individuals have asked me, "Bishop, isn't it a burden to know about other people's sins? Doesn't it get you down—especially to be aware of their serious sins?" My answer is always, "No, it is not a burden, for it is not *my* burden. The weight of their sins is not mine to carry. Jesus Christ paid the ransom for us all. I rejoice when someone wants to repent and to be made clean again. I know the peace and happiness they will enjoy."

While it is always better not to sin, it is a great day when those who have transgressed the commandments desire to return to the Lord, repent of their sins, and be healed (see 3 Nephi 9:13). "We should," explained the father in the parable of the prodigal son, "make merry, and be glad" when someone guilty of sin seeks forgiveness, for "thy brother was dead" and can now be made "alive again" (Luke 15:32).

"We are disposed," stated Joseph Smith, "to look with compassion on perishing souls; we feel that we want to take them upon our shoulders, and cast their sins behind our backs."[1] How true! What a blessing it is to help "lift up the hands which hang down, and strengthen the feeble knees" (D&C 81:5)—to assist those who are exhausted and discouraged by sin and who want to come unto the Savior!

WHAT IS SIN?

Not every wrong we commit is a sin or is sinful. Some wrongs, even those that are serious and perhaps followed by serious consequences, are errors in judgment; they are mistakes.[2] Sin is "the transgression of the law" (1 John 3:4)—the willful violation of any of God's commandments to any degree when we are both "accountable and capable" (Moroni 8:10). We are accountable when we are able to distinguish between right and wrong; we are capable when we know and understand the commandments and are free to exercise our agency. We cannot sin unless we are "capable of repentance" (D&C 20:71).

The number and types of sin seem to be endless. King Benjamin warned, "I cannot tell you all the things whereby ye may commit sin; . . . I cannot number them" (Mosiah 4:29). Satan will tempt us in every way imaginable. But the Lord will not allow us to be tempted above what we are able to bear (see 1 Corinthians 10:13). And when we take "the Holy Spirit for [our] guide" (D&C 45:57), we will be protected from spiritual harm. The Holy Ghost will warn us before we make a wrong choice. I have been told many times by those who are confessing their sins, "The Spirit told me, 'Stop! Don't do it.' But I didn't listen."

SINS OF OMISSION ARE SINS TOO

Not only did the Savior do no wrong, but He also did everything right. We, on the other hand, frequently concern ourselves only with sins of commission (doing something we should not) and less with sins of omission (not doing something we should). As we become perfected in Christ, we stop doing the things we shouldn't be doing and start doing more of the things we should. For example, after we "cease to be covetous" (D&C 88:123) of our neighbors' successes, we are able to "clothe [ourselves] with the bond of charity" (D&C 88:125) and rejoice in their achievements.

There are numerous good works we are commanded to do, such as regular prayer and scripture study, loving and serving others (including home and visiting teaching), assisting in the redemption of the dead, and sharing the gospel. In a quarterly conference John Taylor, then President of the Quorum of the Twelve, warned the priesthood holders: "If you do not magnify your callings, God will hold you responsible for those whom you might have saved had you done your duty."[3] The young men of the Church have a specific duty to share the gospel by serving a mission. President Thomas S. Monson stated:

> I repeat what prophets have long taught—that every worthy, able young man should prepare to serve a mission. Missionary service is a priesthood duty—an obligation the Lord expects of us who have been given so very much.[4]

We are a covenant people and covenant to do good.[5] When we neglect our obligations, we commit sins of omission and need to repent. "To him that knoweth to do good, and doeth it not," wrote James, "to him it is sin" (James 4:17).

THE MAGNITUDE OF SINS

Not all sins are the same—some are certainly more serious than others. And the severity of a specific sin can vary depending on our individual situation. Consequently, our Father in Heaven, who is a just God, treats us differently according to our circumstances. The conditions of our repentance may differ dramatically from the conditions required of someone else—even for the same sin. Here are a few reasons why.

Gospel Knowledge

The more we know and understand the gospel of Jesus Christ, the more we are held accountable for our sinful actions. The Lord pointedly said, "He who sins against the greater light shall receive the greater condemnation" (D&C 82:3). Expounding on this doctrine, Jesus taught His disciples:

> And that servant, which knew his lord's will, and . . . did [not] according to his will, shall be beaten with many stripes. But he that knew not, and did commit things worthy of stripes, shall be beaten with few stripes. For unto whomsoever much is given, of him shall be much required. (Luke 12:47–48)

Sacred Covenants

We are more accountable for our transgressions after we have made sacred covenants.[6] For example, having sexual relations outside the bonds of marriage is a greater sin if we are married (adultery) than if we are single (fornication) because of the marriage covenant; it is a more serious sin if we have received the temple endowment than if we are unbaptized and just beginning to learn the gospel.

The following story illustrates this principle. A few weeks after Claire and her nonmember boyfriend, Tom, moved into the ward, Tom started to take the missionary discussions. It wasn't long before he desired to be baptized. But since they lived together, he first needed to repent and demonstrate his commitment to keep the commandments—either by marrying Claire or by moving somewhere else. Since they were very much in love, Tom and Claire decided to get married. An hour after their wedding ceremony, Tom was baptized. His repentance was now complete, but hers was just beginning.

Premeditation

Our sins are magnified if we plan them in advance—if they are deliberate and premeditated. The book of Proverbs lists a "heart that deviseth wicked imaginations" (Proverbs 6:18) as one of the "six things [that] the Lord hate[s]" (Proverbs 6:16).

For example, if we knowingly accept too much change from a store clerk after making a purchase, we are stealing from the business. Intentionally shoplifting an item is also stealing, but it is much more egregious.

Repetition

We are under greater condemnation if we repeat our transgressions, particularly if we repeat them after learning gospel truths, repenting, and making covenants to live righteously. The Apostle Peter described the state of those who return to their old sins:

> For if after they have escaped the pollutions of the world through the knowledge of the Lord and Saviour Jesus Christ, they are again entangled therein, and overcome, the latter end is worse with them than the beginning. (2 Peter 2:20)

Responsibility for Others

When we are in a position of authority, such as a parent or leader, we have an obligation to protect others from spiritual harm. We are responsible for their sins if we are negligent in our duty. The Lord warned the parents in Zion to teach their children the gospel; otherwise, "the sin be upon the heads of the parents" (D&C 68:25). Ezekiel, a "watchman" of Israel, was given the same accountability from God:

> I have set thee a watchman unto the house of Israel; therefore thou shalt hear the word at my mouth, and warn them from me.
>
> When I say unto the wicked, O wicked man, thou shalt surely die; if thou dost not speak to warn the wicked from his way, that wicked man shall die in his iniquity; but his blood will I require at thine hand.
>
> Nevertheless, if thou warn the wicked of his way to turn from it; if he do not turn from his way, he shall die in his iniquity; but thou hast delivered thy soul. (Ezekiel 33:7–9)

Sphere of Influence

The seriousness of our sins also increases as our importance and influence in society increases. In our larger sphere of influence, our transgressions can directly harm more innocent people. Our sins gain wider exposure and can turn more individuals away from the truth and from their Savior Jesus Christ. Mosiah taught his people, "The sins of many people have been caused by the iniquities of their kings; therefore their iniquities are answered upon the heads of their kings" (Mosiah 29:31).

THE LAW OF CHASTITY

Some of the most serious and pervasive sins in the world today are transgressions of the law of chastity. Unfortunately, they are also almost universally accepted and even applauded and celebrated. President Ezra Taft Benson, speaking of the scourge of sexual sin in our day, said,

> The plaguing sin of this generation is sexual immorality. This, the Prophet Joseph said, would be the source of more temptations, more buffetings, and more difficulties for the elders of Israel than any other.[7]

My wife wrote of a poignant experience she had years ago that illustrates the consequences of both keeping and breaking the law of chastity:

> Shortly after I arrived in the waiting room for my doctor's appointment, a woman from our ward, who had finished seeing her doctor, came into the lobby where I was sitting. As I stood to greet her, she was quick to announce, "I'm pregnant!" We embraced as I congratulated her on her wonderful news. She and her husband were finally going to have a baby!
>
> After our brief exchange I continued to wait for my appointment. To my surprise, an unwed woman in her twenties, also from our ward, finished her appointment and entered the waiting room. I could see her eyes were red and swollen. She came toward me and in a soft, halting voice shared her news, "I'm pregnant." She was reeling from shock, uncertainty, and despair. She desperately needed a shoulder to cry on. We embraced and wept together.

Sexual sins are extremely destructive to our spiritual and emotional well-being. They can destroy marriages and families. They are some of the most serious of all sins. Alma taught his son Corianton that sexual immorality was the "most abominable above all sins save it be the shedding of innocent blood or denying the Holy Ghost" (Alma 39:5). Are sexual sins really that serious? Yes, they are. To repeat, the three most serious sins, in order of magnitude, are denying the Holy Ghost,[8] murder, and sexual immorality (meaning sexual relations other than those between a man and a woman who are legally married to each other[9]).

Far too many individuals minimize the seriousness of sexual transgressions. After my daughter, Kristi, discussed the law of chastity with a friend, he commented, "You have really high standards." She responded, "These aren't my standards; they're the Lord's standards!" And, indeed, they are.

The Lord's standard for sexual purity is complete chastity before marriage and total fidelity after marriage. Complete chastity before marriage means we should not dwell on or entertain immoral thoughts, be immodest (in dress, behavior—including some forms of dancing—and conversation), share sexually explicit images of ourselves, view pornography, masturbate, kiss passionately (including French or tongue kissing), touch or fondle another person's private body parts (whether clothed or unclothed), perform oral sex, have sexual intercourse, or engage in homosexual relations.

After marriage, husbands and wives are to love each other with all their hearts and to "cleave unto [each other] and none else" (D&C 42:22). We should never do anything that calls into question our faithfulness to our spouse or that is adulterous in any manner (see Matthew 5:28).

Tragically, sexual immorality can also precede another grave sin—unjustified, elective abortion. The Lord warned, "Thou shalt not . . . kill, nor do anything like unto it" (D&C 59:6).

The Lord continually invites us to repent. He knows all our transgressions in all their varied degrees, and He is willing to cleanse us of each and every one when we come unto Him and partake of His redeeming power.

NOTES

1. Joseph Smith, *History of the Church of Jesus Christ of Latter-day Saints* (Salt Lake City: The Church of Jesus Christ of Latter-day Saints, 1949), 5:24.

2. See Dallin H. Oaks, "Sins and Mistakes," *Ensign*, October 1996, 62–67.

3. John Taylor, in *Journal of Discourses* (London: Latter-day Saints' Book Depot, 1880), 20:23.

4. Thomas S. Monson, "As We Meet Together Again," *Ensign*, November 2010, 5–6.

5. See Boyd K. Packer, *The Holy Temple* (Salt Lake City: Bookcraft, 1980), 170.

6. We enter into covenants through ordinances such as baptism, ordination to the Melchizedek Priesthood, and the temple endowment.

7. Ezra Taft Benson, "Cleansing the Inner Vessel," *Ensign*, May 1986, 4.

8. Denying the Holy Ghost is the unforgivable sin of opposing Jesus Christ after having direct personal knowledge of His existence. Those who commit this sin become sons of perdition.

9. See The First Presidency and Council of the Twelve Apostles, "The Family: A Proclamation to the World," *Ensign*, November 1995, 102.

The CONSEQUENCES *of* SIN

SOMETIMES, WHILE WE are sinning, we convince ourselves that there are no consequences to our sins, or we hope that the consequences will never happen. But "the consequences of sin" (2 Nephi 9:48) are real. Each one is harmful and destructive, and each one will separate us "from that which is good" (2 Nephi 2:5)—either now or in the future. Fortunately, most of them can be overcome through repentance, but, sadly, some of the consequences of sin are permanent.

SEPARATION FROM GOD AND ETERNAL PROGRESSION

If we are not "cleansed from all [our] sins" (D&C 76:52) and "made perfect through Jesus" (D&C 76:69), we cannot live with God in celestial glory, "worlds without end" (D&C 76:112). The scriptures are replete with warnings, including the following:

> The kingdom of God is not filthy, and there cannot any unclean thing enter into the kingdom of God. (1 Nephi 15:34)

> Except he repenteth . . . [he] hath no interest in the kingdom of God. (Mosiah 4:18)

> Inasmuch as ye will not keep my commandments ye shall be cut off from my presence. (2 Nephi 1:20)

Without repentance, our opportunities for eternal progression will also come to an end. We will never receive "all that [our] Father hath" (D&C 84:38) or be "crowned with honor, and glory, and immortality, and eternal life" (D&C 75:5). We will never hear the Lord's sublime words: "Well done, good and faithful servant; thou hast been faithful over a few things, I will make thee ruler over many things: enter thou into the joy of thy lord" (Matthew 25:23).

SEPARATION FROM FAMILY

President Ezra Taft Benson, in expressing his desire to live eternally with his family, said in general conference, "As parents and grandparents in Zion, it has been the shared hope of my wife and me that all of us will be together in the eternities—that all will be worthy, without a single empty chair."[1]

If we have not repented of all our transgressions, we cannot join our righteous family members in the celestial kingdom of God. Our eternal marriage under the new and everlasting covenant will be revoked, and the sealing ties binding us to our parents and to our children will be severed. We will be separate and single throughout all eternity (see D&C 132:17).

SEPARATION FROM THE HOLY GHOST

Our sins can separate us from the companionship of the Holy Ghost. "My Spirit," warned the Lord, "shall not always strive with man" (D&C 1:33). The Spirit will continue to be with us when we repent. But if we persist in our iniquities, we become "filthy and polluted" (Zephaniah 3:1); we become unholy. The Holy Ghost soon departs from us, and we are left alone "because the Spirit of the Lord doth not dwell in unholy temples" (Helaman 4:24). Mormon described how the fluctuating obedience of the Nephites and the Lamanites affected their ability to receive the Spirit:

> The Spirit of the Lord began to withdraw from the Nephites, because of the wickedness and the hardness of their hearts. And . . . the Lord began to pour out his Spirit upon the Lamanites, because of their easiness and willingness to believe in his words. (Helaman 6:35–36)

We lose an "unspeakable gift" (D&C 121:26) when the Holy Ghost is withheld from us. We are no longer entitled to receive personal revelation or to feel of God's love, joy, and peace—"the fruit[s] of the Spirit" (Galatians 5:22). The Lord, in order to help Martin Harris understand the much greater suffering he would receive if he did not repent, reminded him how he felt when he lost the companionship of the Holy Ghost: "Repent, . . . lest you suffer these punishments of which I have spoken, of which in the smallest, yea, even in the least degree you have tasted at the time I withdrew my Spirit" (D&C 19:20).

Some years ago I received a letter from a former member of the Church. In it he described how he had "tasted" the complete withdrawal of the Spirit because of his wickedness and subsequent excommunication:

> It is final now. I am an ex-Mormon. . . . When the Spirit withdrew it was like a cold shudder that left me confused and bewildered. . . . The withdrawal was a tangible experience that verged on pain. I cried. . . . I feel so empty.[2]

SEPARATION FROM KNOWLEDGE

Without the Spirit of the Lord, we lose by degrees spiritual knowledge, testimony, and ultimately faith. Fundamental doctrines become fuzzy. We begin to question principles we once held dear. Our trust in ecclesiastical leaders lessens. We begin "to disbelieve in the spirit of prophecy and in the spirit of revelation" (Helaman 4:23). We question the Lord and His purposes. We even question His existence. Our minds become "darkened because of unbelief" (D&C 84:54), and we end up "walking in darkness at noon-day" (D&C 95:6). The Lord warned, "He that repents not, from him shall be taken even the light which he has received" (D&C 1:33). And Alma testified, "They that will harden their hearts, to them is given the lesser portion of the word until they know nothing concerning his mysteries" (Alma 12:11).

We probably all know or are aware of members who once had strong testimonies of the gospel and were fully active in the Church. But then "pride and the cares of the world" (D&C 39:9) took priority in their lives, and they began to commit sins of omission—they neglected to say their prayers or to read the scriptures. They stopped fulfilling their Church callings and eventually no longer came to church. After committing sins of omission, some of them found it easy to commit sins of commission, such as breaking the Word of Wisdom or violating the law of chastity. As the Spirit of the Lord continued to withdraw from them, they were often "blinded by the craftiness of men" (D&C 76:75) and found "the things of the Spirit of God" to be "foolishness" (1 Corinthians 2:14).

SEPARATION FROM THE CHURCH

Our wickedness can separate us from our privileges of Church membership[3] or even from our membership itself. Severe Church discipline, such as disfellowshipment and excommunication, is administered by priesthood leaders in love and as guided by the Spirit.

The primary purpose of Church discipline is to save souls. Church discipline helps members who have committed serious sins recognize the need to make significant changes in their lives and to repent. The Lord told Alma, "Whosoever will not repent of his sins the same shall not be numbered among my people." Therefore, "Alma went and judged those that had been taken in iniquity. . . . And those that would not confess their sins and repent of their iniquity, the same were not numbered among the people of the church, and their names were blotted out" (Mosiah 26:32, 34, 36). The Lord gave the same instruction to His servants in our dispensation, saying, "He that receiveth my law . . . and doeth it not, the same is not my disciple, and shall be cast out [excommunicated]" (D&C 41:5).[4]

SEPARATION FROM BLESSINGS

God withholds blessings from us when we are disobedient. He declared, "I, the Lord, am bound when ye do what I say; but when ye do not what I say, ye have no promise" (D&C 82:10). He cannot, He will not, reward wickedness. "I will not succor my people," said the Lord, "in the day of their transgression; but I will hedge up their ways that they prosper not" (Mosiah 7:29). If we want to receive a blessing from the Lord, we must "abide the law which was appointed for that blessing" (D&C 132:5).

We can permanently lose some blessings as a consequence of our wickedness. I once visited with a member of the Church who told me the eternal price he paid for his continued transgressions. Many years prior to our conversation he had been sealed in the temple to his wonderful wife and beautiful children. Unfortunately, sometime after receiving his temple blessings he succumbed to an old drug habit and became inactive in the Church. He promised his wife he would turn his life around and return to church, but he was unsuccessful in doing so. The years passed by, and after much struggle and hardship, his wife divorced him. She later received a cancellation of their sealing and was sealed to someone else. At last he overcame his addiction, repented of his sins, and felt the sweet spirit of forgiveness from the Lord. He returned to full activity in the Church (and, in fact, was serving as a temple ordinance worker when he moved into the ward). He had been forgiven of his sins, yet all his prior blessings could not be restored—he had forever lost his wife, who was once his eternal companion.

This man's story has an important element in common with the story of the prodigal son. "Forgiveness," observed Elder Spencer W. Kimball, "can never restore the losses he [the repentant sinner] sustained during the period of his sinning."[5]

SEPARATION FROM AGENCY

Satan will try to fool us into thinking we have more freedom when we are sinning than when we are obeying the commandments. We don't. The Lord has given us our agency to choose between good and evil, but each time we choose evil our subsequent choices, without repentance, become more limited. Satan will lead us "by the neck with a flaxen cord, until he bindeth [us] with his strong cords forever" (2 Nephi 26:22). In fact, his strong cords become "the chains of hell," and we are then "taken captive by the devil, and led by his will down to destruction" (Alma 12:11). We will, in our final and terrible state as transgressors, have completely forfeited our agency. The Spirit of the Lord will have ceased striving with us (see Ether 15:19), and the devil "doth seal [us] his" and has "all power over [us]" (Alma 34:35). Our salvation in the kingdom of God is now no longer possible, for "it is everlastingly too late, and [our] destruction is made sure" (Helaman 13:38).

SEPARATION FROM HAPPINESS

The Lord wants us to be happy; it is one of the purposes of life. Lehi taught, "Men are, that they might have joy" (2 Nephi 2:25). Real happiness—true, complete peace and contentment, and full confidence before God—is one of the greatest blessings of keeping the commandments. It is happiness that only comes through righteous living and from being clean.

The devil, on the other hand, wants us to be "miserable like unto himself" (2 Nephi 2:27). Satan fully understands "wickedness never was happiness" (Alma 41:10). He can destroy our happiness if we yield to his temptations and transgress the laws of God. "The wicked," the Lord said, "are like the troubled sea, when it cannot rest, whose waters cast up mire and dirt" (Isaiah 57:20).

A young adult once told me during an interview, "I don't know what I was thinking. I thought I'd find happiness by going out and drinking with some of my friends after work. And I did for a short period of time. But now I'm not happy at all."

God may allow us "to enjoy the pleasures of sin for a season" (Hebrews 11:25), but we must be careful not to seek "all the days of [our] lives for that which [we cannot] obtain . . . happiness in doing iniquity" (Helaman 13:38). It cannot be done; it is contrary to the order of heaven. Do not trade your inheritance in the kingdom of God—where your "joy shall be full forever" (2 Nephi 9:18)—for today's temporary worldly pleasures.

NOTES

1. Ezra Taft Benson, "Counsel to the Saints," *Ensign*, May 1984, 7.
2. Personal correspondence.
3. These include partaking of the sacrament, exercising the priesthood, serving in a Church position, giving talks or prayers in Church meetings, participating in the sustaining of Church officers, and entering the temple.
4. Note, however, "ye shall not cast him out of your . . . places of worship, for unto such shall ye continue to minister; for ye know

not but what they will return and repent, and come unto me with full purpose of heart, and I shall heal them; and ye shall be the means of bringing salvation unto them" (3 Nephi 18:32).

5. Spencer W. Kimball, *The Miracle of Forgiveness* (Salt Lake City: Bookcraft, 1969), 311.

The VOICE *of* WARNING

*I*N OUR PREMORTAL life, as God's spirit children, we rejoiced at the opportunity to come to earth to gain physical bodies and progress toward eternal life. After Jesus Christ, the Firstborn in the spirit (see D&C 93:21), had "laid the foundations of the earth" (Job 38:4), "the morning stars sang together, and all the sons of God shouted for joy" (Job 38:7).

Satan, known as Lucifer, was there also, for he too is one of God's spirit children. He was "a son of the morning" (D&C 76:26) and "an angel of God who was in authority in the presence of God" (D&C 76:25).

Contrary to Heavenly Father's plan for our salvation, Satan proposed his idea to save each of us by telling God, "I will be thy son, and I will redeem all mankind" (Moses 4:1). Lucifer's plan was one of compulsion. He wanted "to destroy the agency of man" (Moses 4:3)—our gift from God to act for ourselves and to make our own choices. In return for his promise not to lose a single soul, Lucifer demanded of our Father, "Give me thine honor" (D&C 29:36), which is God's power. His true ambition was to exalt his "throne above the stars of God" and to "be like the most High" (Isaiah 14:13–14).

Our Father in Heaven rejected Satan's proposal and accepted the offer of Jesus Christ (see Abraham 3:27), His "Beloved and Chosen from the beginning" (Moses 4:2), to bring about His plan for our redemption and exaltation.

Angered at his rejection, Satan rebelled against God and Jesus Christ. In his rebellion—and true to his desire to reign supreme—he sought "the throne of him who sitteth upon the throne, even the Lamb" (D&C 88:115) and "to take the kingdom of our God and his Christ" (D&C 76:28).

Satan endeavored to persuade us to follow him, and he became "the accuser of our brethren . . . before our God day and night" (Revelation 12:10). As the accuser, he undoubtedly slandered or found fault with the righteous followers of Christ or of the Savior Himself. He was, after all, "a liar from the beginning" (D&C 93:25), and there was "no truth in him" (John 8:44). Perhaps Satan questioned the capacity of Jesus Christ to fulfill the Atonement or, like his false accusation against Job (see Job 1:11; 2:5), the ability of "the noble and great ones" (Abraham 3:22) to remain righteous in this life.

While Satan reviled against the righteous sons and daughters of God, he certainly also flattered God's prideful children with a promise to "make them rulers over the people" (Alma 46:5) after he overthrew our Father's kingdom. And, of course, he deceitfully preached of the necessity and the superiority of his proposal to all who would listen—guaranteeing he would save everyone while arguing God could or would not.

Thus there was a war in heaven—a war over eternal truths and lies, over freedom of choice and forced obedience, and over Satan's struggle for power and his desire to overthrow God and reign in His stead. And, most important, the War in Heaven was over the souls of men—Christ and His followers (notably Adam) on one side, and Satan and his followers on the other. The war lasted at least until we all decided whom to follow. It ended with the expulsion of Satan and his followers from heaven:

> Michael [Adam, the archangel] and his angels fought against the dragon; and the dragon fought and his angels, and prevailed not; neither was their place found any more in heaven.
>
> And the great dragon was cast out, that old serpent, called the Devil, and Satan, which deceiveth the whole world: he was cast out into the earth, and his angels [the third part of the stars of heaven (Revelation 12:4)] were cast out with him. (Revelation 12:7–9)

Satan and his followers were cast down to earth by the power of God's Only Begotten Son (see Moses 4:3). And though the "heavens wept over [Satan]" (D&C 76:26), there was "a loud voice saying in heaven, Now is come salvation, and strength, and the kingdom of our God, and the power of his Christ: for the accuser of our brethren is cast down" (Revelation 12:10). The plan of salvation could now commence, and we could begin our journey toward eternal life. Certainly we rejoiced again!

SATAN HATH DESIRED TO HAVE YOU

A primary purpose of our earthly existence is to prove us, to see if we will obey all God's commandments (see Abraham 3:25). Part of our testing is a result of Satan's continued war against us, for "it must needs be that the devil should tempt the children of men, or they could not be agents unto themselves" (D&C 29:39). Satan's intent is "to deceive and to blind [us], and to lead [us] captive at his will" (Moses 4:4). Jesus told Simon Peter, "Satan hath desired to have you, that he may sift you as wheat: But I have prayed for thee, that thy faith fail not" (Luke 22:31–32).

Satan is real. His power is real. He is "an enemy to all righteousness" (Alma 34:23). He is our avowed enemy. He "goeth up and down, to and fro in the earth, seeking to destroy the souls of men" (D&C 10:27). He hates us and wants to destroy us. He is "as a roaring lion, walk[ing] about, seeking whom he may devour" (1 Peter 5:8).

Satan wants us to be as miserable as he is. His mission is our complete and utter unhappiness and failure; he wants us eternally estranged from God. He will "laugh, and his angels rejoice" (Moses 7:26; tense changed) if we become a casualty of the war—unable to return to God because of unworthiness. He will count our capture as a success against his ultimate enemies, God and Jesus Christ.

An experience recorded by Heber C. Kimball illustrates this truth. On July 30, 1837, in Preston, England, Elder Kimball was attacked by evil spirits while giving a blessing to his fellow missionary, Elder Isaac Russel. Elder Kimball saw the evil spirits in a vision and later wrote,

I was struck with great force by some invisible power, and fell sense-less on the floor; and the first thing I recollected was being sup-ported by Elders Hyde and Russel who were praying for me. They then laid me on the bed, but my agony was so great I arose, bowed on my knees and prayed.

I then sat on the bed and could distinctly see the evil spir-its who foamed and gnashed their teeth upon us. We gazed upon them about an hour and a half, . . . and we saw the devils coming in legions with their leaders, who came within a few feet of us, they came towards us like armies rushing to battle, they appeared men of full stature, possessing every . . . appearance of men in the flesh, . . . who were angry and desperate, and I shall never forget the vindictive malignity depicted on their countenances, and any attempt to paint the scene which then presented itself; or portray the malice and enmity depicted in their countenances would be vain. I perspired exceedingly, and my clothes were as wet as if I had been taken out of the river.

Although I felt excessive pain, and was in the greatest distress for some time, and cannot even look back on the scene without feelings of horror; yet, by it I learned the power of the adversary, his enmity against the servants of God, and got some understanding of the invisible world. We distinctly heard those spirits talk and express their wrath and hellish designs against us. However the Lord delivered us from them, and blessed us exceedingly that day.[1]

A DAY OF WARNING

In our pre-earth life, Jesus undoubtedly invited us to follow Him and warned us of the eternal consequences in yielding to Satan—just as He does now. Today, in particular, is "a day of warning" (D&C 63:58), for "tomorrow all the proud and they that do wickedly" (D&C 64:24) will be as stubble and burned.

If we are humble, we are "acceptable before God" (Moroni 7:44), and His "grace is sufficient" (Ether 12:26) for us. But if we are pride-ful, the Lord's "anger is kindled against [us]" (D&C 63:2) because we are in "open rebellion" against Him and have chosen to "obey the evil spirit" (Mosiah 2:37).

Thus, we are warned lest we are unhappily counted among the unrighteous of this world when God's wrath will "be poured out upon the wicked without measure" (D&C 1:9). It will be a day of calamity, tribulation, and desolation (see D&C 1:17; 29:8). Peace will "be taken from the earth, and the devil shall have power over his own dominion" (D&C 1:35). The Saints will "hardly escape" (D&C 63:34), but God "will preserve the righteous by his power. . . . Wherefore, the righteous need not fear" (1 Nephi 22:17).

We are also warned that we will be "brought before the bar of God" and "judged according to our works" (Alma 12:12). If we have not repented of all our sins, our earlier shouts for joy in the premortal existence will turn into "weeping, wailing and gnashing of teeth" (D&C 19:5). Instead of being a "glorious day when justice shall be administered unto the righteous" (2 Nephi 9:46), our Judgment Day will provide us with "an awful view of [our] guilt and abominations" (Mosiah 3:25). We will "quake, and tremble, and shrink beneath the glance of [the Lord's] all-searching eye" (Mosiah 27:31). We will "not dare to look up to our God; and we would fain be glad if we could command the rocks and the mountains to fall upon us to hide us from his presence" (Alma 12:14).

Enos, along with other prophets, warned the people of his day in a manner similar to the warnings of our day:

> And there was nothing save it was exceeding harshness, preaching and prophesying of wars, and contentions, and destructions, and continually reminding them of death, and the duration of eternity, and the judgments and the power of God . . . to keep them . . . from going down speedily to destruction. (Enos 1:23)

We have been warned—clearly and unequivocally. If we heed the Lord's warnings and repent of our sins, we will be spared the punishments reserved for the wicked and receive all the blessings promised to the faithful.

ETERNAL PUNISHMENT AND THE RESURRECTION

Several years ago I began to meet regularly with a less-active sister in our ward. After a period of time, this sweet, humble woman was able to repent of her sins. Shortly thereafter she passed away. While her death was sudden and unexpected, I was grateful she was able to leave this world "prepared to meet God" (Alma 5:28).

Her funeral service was solemn yet upbeat. Funerals are always tearful good-byes, but services for those who have died "firm in the faith of Christ" (Alma 27:27) are also comforting and uplifting. We rejoice knowing our deceased family members and friends are worthy to inherit eternal glory, and our separation, if we remain faithful, will end with a joyful reunion. "Thou shalt weep," stated the Lord, "for the loss of them that die, and more especially for those that have not hope of a glorious resurrection" (D&C 42:45).

A glorious resurrection awaits us after we have accepted the gospel of Jesus Christ (see D&C 76:50–53, 82) and have "been faithful in the testimony of Jesus" (D&C 138:12). We will rise in the morning of the resurrection of the just to inherit the celestial kingdom. But if we fail to keep our covenants and do not repent of our sins, we will, after this life, find ourselves in spirit prison, paying "the penalty of [our] transgressions" (D&C 138:59) and coming forth in a later resurrection.

If we have not been "valiant in the testimony of Jesus" (D&C 76:79), we will, along with the "honorable men of the earth" (D&C 76:75), come forth in the afternoon of the resurrection of the just to dwell in the terrestrial kingdom. And if we are wicked, we will join all the other wicked and rise in the resurrection of the unjust to inherit either the telestial kingdom or outer darkness (perdition).

The wicked—those who have been "warned of their iniquities and . . . would not depart from them" (Mosiah 16:12), who receive "not the gospel, neither the testimony of Jesus, neither the prophets" (D&C 76:101), and who are unrepentant "liars, and sorcerers, and adulterers, and whoremongers" (D&C 76:103)—will pay the full cost of all their iniquities. They "must suffer even as" (D&C 19:17) the Lord suffered. They will "suffer the wrath of God on earth" (D&C 76:104) and "are cast down to hell and suffer the wrath of Almighty God, until the fulness of times" (D&C 76:106). In other words, they remain in hell, or spirit prison, to pay the awful penalty for their own sins until they are "redeemed from the devil" (D&C 76:85) when "the thousand years are ended" (D&C 88:101).

Although their punishment is termed "endless," it is not endless in duration. Hell "must deliver up its captive spirits" (2 Nephi 9:12). The Lord explained:

> It is not written that there shall be no end to this torment, but it is written *endless torment*. Again, it is written *eternal damnation*; wherefore it is more express than other scriptures, that it might work upon the hearts of the children of men, altogether for my name's glory. . . .
>
> For, behold, I am endless, and the punishment which is given from my hand is endless punishment, for Endless is my name. Wherefore—Eternal punishment is God's punishment. Endless punishment is God's punishment. (D&C 19:6–7, 10–12; emphasis in original)

Satan, his angels, and the sons of perdition[2] will be consigned to everlasting and eternal punishment in outer darkness (see D&C 76:44). This is the true definition of hell, and it has no end.

Even though the unrighteous fulfill the demands of justice by paying the debt for their own sins, they cannot inherit the celestial kingdom, "worlds without end" (D&C 76:112). They have not "become the sons of God" (Moroni 7:48), nor have they become like Him. In fact, they "would be more miserable to dwell with a holy and just God, under a consciousness of [their] filthiness before him, than [they] would to dwell with the damned souls in hell" (Mormon 9:4).

HE THAT RECEIVETH ME

Jesus Christ willingly and humbly accepted His all-encompassing role in God's plan for our salvation. He came to save us. He promises the faithful they will "receive their inheritance and be made equal with him" (D&C 88:107) and enjoy all that our Father in Heaven enjoys:

> For he that receiveth my servants receiveth me; and he that receiveth me receiveth my Father; and he that receiveth my Father receiveth my Father's kingdom; therefore all that my Father hath shall be given unto him. (D&C 84:36–38)

Satan, on the other hand, has never stopped opposing God and His plan for us. Ruled by pride, he sought and fought for our Heavenly Father's kingdom in the pre-earth life and is still fighting for it today, but the kingdom will be given to all who humbly and righteously follow God's plan. Satan will ultimately lose the war, and his final condemnation will be to "a kingdom which is not a kingdom of glory" (D&C 88:24). There he will suffer everlasting punishment and torment—"the end, the width, the height, the depth, and the misery thereof" (D&C 76:48) we cannot comprehend.

Satan's plan for our salvation would never have worked. We need our agency to progress. The Lord teaches us the proper use of our agency through the gospel of Jesus Christ, and He warns us against its misuse. Heeding the Lord's warnings today is just as vital to our eternal progression as it was in our premortal existence.

NOTES

1. Heber C. Kimball, "Synopsis of the History of Heber Chase Kimball," *The Deseret News*, April 21, 1858, 37.
2. Sons of perdition are those who have denied both "the Holy Spirit after having received it" (D&C 76:35) and "the Son after the Father has revealed him" (D&C 76:43). They are the last to be resurrected and "shall remain filthy still" (D&C 88:102).

NOW IS *the* TIME *to* REPENT

*I*N MY CONVERSATION with a middle-aged father about his disobedience to one of God's commandments, he repeatedly told me, "Bishop, you don't understand." I obviously wasn't being successful in convincing him to repent and to do so immediately. The true meaning of his statement was: "I'm an exception to the rule. The commandment we are talking about doesn't apply to me right now because of my circumstances." Unfortunately, he hasn't been the only one to reject an invitation to repent. Other members I have counseled have also justified their continued disobedience:

"I have to take this job even though it requires me to work on Sundays, so I don't know when I'll be back to church."

"It's cheaper for us to live together, so that's what we have to do. But we'll be married soon."

"My bills are more than I make, so there's no way I can pay my tithing right now."

These members decided it was safe for them to procrastinate their repentance. But it is never safe. Alma, in response to the people of Ammonihah who also felt no need to repent immediately, pleaded in "a mighty voice," saying,

> Now is the time to repent, for the day of salvation draweth nigh; . . . I wish from the inmost part of my heart, yea, with great anxiety even unto pain, that ye would hearken unto my words,

and cast off your sins, and not procrastinate the day of your repentance. (Alma 13:21, 27)

Why did Alma declare repentance with such great urgency and anxiety? Because he knew the people of Ammonihah would soon be destroyed if they did not quickly repent—bringing an end to both their lives and their opportunity for eternal life. Alma's great love for others was like that of the sons of Mosiah, who "could not bear that any human soul should perish; yea, even the very thoughts that any soul should endure endless torment did cause them to quake and tremble" (Mosiah 28:3).

One of Satan's many deceptions is to persuade us to delay our repentance. President Joseph Fielding Smith stated, "Procrastination, as it may be applied to gospel principles, is the thief of eternal life."[1] If we are not careful, we may find we have postponed our repentance until it is too late and the gates of the celestial kingdom are no longer open to us. In the parable of the ten virgins (who represent the members of the Church), Jesus emphasized that we must always be prepared and worthy to meet Him:

Then shall the kingdom of heaven be likened unto ten virgins, which took their lamps, and went forth to meet the bridegroom.

And five of them were wise, and five were foolish. They that were foolish took their lamps, and took no oil with them: but the wise took oil in their vessels with their lamps.

While the bridegroom tarried, they all slumbered and slept. And at midnight there was a cry made, Behold, the bridegroom cometh; go ye out to meet him.

Then all those virgins arose, and trimmed their lamps. And the foolish said unto the wise, Give us of your oil; for our lamps are gone out. But the wise answered, saying, Not so; lest there be not enough for us and you: but go ye rather to them that sell, and buy for yourselves.

And while they went to buy, the bridegroom came; and they that were ready went in with him to the marriage: and the door was shut. Afterward came also the other virgins, saying, Lord, Lord, open to us. But he answered and said, Verily I say unto you, I know you not.

Watch therefore, for ye know neither the day nor the hour wherein the Son of man cometh. (Matthew 25:1–13)

As the foolish virgins painfully learned, now is the time to prepare and repent. The prophet Joshua challenged the Israelites to "choose you *this day* whom ye will serve" (Joshua 24:15; emphasis added). We cannot afford to wait "lest death shall overtake [us]; in an hour when [we] think not the summer shall be past, and the harvest ended, and [our] souls not saved" (D&C 45:2).

THE DESTRUCTIVE EFFECTS OF PROCRASTINATION

The longer we postpone our repentance, the more spiritually weakened we become. Our confidence in our ability to keep the commandments may fade. Our feelings of self-worth may decrease, and our "hope of a glorious resurrection" (D&C 138:14) may slip away. Our trust in the Lord's love for us and His willingness to heal and redeem us may falter.

As we continue to sin, it becomes more difficult for us to put off "the natural man" and to become "a saint through the atonement of Christ the Lord" (Mosiah 3:19). The Spirit begins to withdraw, and we may lose the motivation and strength we need to change. Our hearts may become hardened, and we may no longer consider our sinful actions to be evil. We may even arrive at the point where we "call evil good, and good evil" (Isaiah 5:20).

The longer we wait to repent, the more blessings we will forfeit—both today and perhaps for all eternity.

I DELAYED NOT

We should always respond to the Lord's command to repent by saying, "I made haste, and delayed not to keep thy commandments" (Psalm 119:60). We really have no legitimate excuse to procrastinate our repentance. Yet many times we convince ourselves that our procrastination is justified. Our excuses, like all excuses for delay, ultimately do not matter—our progress is still stopped. What matters, then, is that we identify and remove the root causes that are keeping us from repenting. Below are three questions that can help us discover why we are delaying our repentance (these are also the first three conditions of repentance discussed in the next section).

Do I Have Pride?

We may not want to let go of our sins because we are enjoying "pleasure in wickedness" (Psalm 5:4) and plan to repent later—a dangerous strategy and a significant misunderstanding of the Atonement. Maybe, because of pride, we want to remain in our anger or continue to be offended. Pride may also make us embarrassed and concerned with what others will think of us if we confess our sins; it will defend us as we rationalize our sins or blame others for our actions.

Pride can make us lazy or indifferent and lull us "away into carnal security." We may tell ourselves, "All is well" (2 Nephi 28:21), or say, "Someday, I will repent." But if that day never arrives, we may try to excuse our inaction by erroneously hoping that God's mercy will rob justice and allow us to enter into His kingdom.

Do I Lack Faith?

Faith is a principle of action.[2] A weak faith in Jesus Christ and a wavering testimony of His Atonement will not provide us the strength we need to change.

We may also, because of our lack of faith, be afraid to repent. Repentance is not easy. The result, however, is true happiness and peace. Do not let fear of one or more of your conditions of repentance, such as confessing your sins, stop you from starting your repentance. Satan wants you to be fearful and discouraged. He wants you to feel it is too late to repent or that repentance is too difficult and you are not "celestial material." Do not believe it! You have a divine heritage and infinite potential. The Lord redeems "as many as will" (Moses 5:9), and when you deny yourself "of all ungodliness . . . then is his grace sufficient for you" (Moroni 10:32).

Do I Lack Knowledge?

We may not recognize our sins. But when we are humble and listen closely, the sins we are committing unknowingly will be brought to our attention by the Spirit, by leaders, friends and family members, and through our study of the scriptures. Paul told the Athenians, "The times of this ignorance God winked at; but now commandeth all men every where to repent" (Acts 17:30). God is calling each of us to repentance, for we all have overlooked or neglected sins that need to be forsaken.

Satan "is the author of all sin" (Helaman 6:30) and of every excuse we use to delay our repentance and cling to our sins. The Lord, of course, encourages us to eliminate our excuses and to summon up the faith and humility we need to start repenting today and to continue through the repentance process until our sins are forgiven.

PREPARE FOR ETERNITY

Amulek, like his missionary companion Alma, implored his listeners to prepare for eternity by repenting today:

> I beseech of you that ye do not procrastinate the day of your repentance until the end; for after this day of life, which is given us to prepare for eternity, behold, if we do not improve our time while in this life, then cometh the night of darkness wherein there can be no labor performed.
>
> Ye cannot say, when ye are brought to that awful crisis, that I will repent, that I will return to my God. Nay, ye cannot say this; for that same spirit which doth possess your bodies at the time that ye go out of this life, that same spirit will have power to possess your body in that eternal world. (Alma 34:33–34)

Some years ago I had a conversation with my son that illustrates the important principle of taking action now to realize our goals for the future. Early in his high school career, Matt came to me one evening and said, "Dad, I need you to help me with my homework tonight." I replied, half teasing, half serious, "I don't want to do homework." "But I need your help," he emphasized. So I asked, "Why do you need my help tonight?" After some thought he answered, "Well, if you help me tonight, I'll understand the assignment, and I'll do well on the test. If I do well on my test, I'll get a good grade in the class. If I get good grades, I'll be able to go to college. If I graduate from college, I'll be able to get a good job. And if I get a good job, I'll be able to support my future family. So I need you to help me tonight!"

We are right now determining our eternal rewards. Now is the time to prepare for eternity. Now is the time to repent. Do not let today slip by. The poet John Whittier, referring to lost opportunities, wrote, "For of all sad words of tongue or pen, The saddest are these: 'It might have been!' "[3]

Peter and Andrew, the early Apostles, "straightway left their nets" (Matthew 4:20) and followed Christ. We too should immediately leave our sins and follow the Savior.

NOTES

1. Joseph Fielding Smith, in Conference Report, April 1969, 121.
2. See Joseph Smith, *Lectures on Faith* (Salt Lake City: Deseret Book, 1985), 1–2.
3. John G. Whittier, *Maud Muller* (Boston: Ticknor and Fields, 1867), 12.

SECTION 3

THE CONDITIONS OF REPENTANCE

ELIMINATING PRIDE:
The DEPTHS *of* HUMILITY

EWARE OF PRIDE," warned the Lord, "lest thou shouldst enter into temptation" (D&C 23:1). Let me illustrate this truth with an experience.

I welcomed a member into my office and invited him to take a seat near my desk. He sat there in silence for a few moments, looking down and shaking his head slowly back and forth. When he composed himself, he said, "I can't believe I'm going to say what I have to say." He was still in disbelief that he was capable of committing the sin to which he was about to confess. After his confession he added these significant words: "I didn't think it would ever happen to me. I thought I was stronger than that."

I have often heard this heartbreaking claim—and its counterpart: "I thought I was smarter than that." These sad and bitter declarations rightfully imply the sin and all its consequences could and should have been avoided.

Those guilty of trusting in "their own strength and upon their own wisdom" (Helaman 16:15)—instead of relying on the Lord—allowed their pride to blind them to their weaknesses. They unwittingly challenged Satan, and he took full advantage of each situation.

Frequently, those who thought they were too strong or too smart to commit a serious sin also confessed to a lesser evil: "We were just going to have a little fun making out," or "I was only going to do drugs with my friends." They thought they could put themselves in a dangerous situation or trifle with risky behavior and still keep from committing a serious transgression. But many times small sins, especially when they are repeated, become big ones; "a little fun" turns into fornication, and "a little drug use" progresses into a heavy drug habit that is difficult to break.

THE SIN OF PRIDE

Pride is a sin and the root of all sins.[1] Pride puts us in conflict with God and His eternal purposes. President Ezra Taft Benson taught, "The central feature of pride is enmity—enmity toward God and enmity toward our fellowmen. *Enmity* means 'hatred toward, hostility to, or a state of opposition.'" He continued, "Pride is essentially competitive in nature. We pit our will against God's." He then added, "Disobedience is essentially a prideful power struggle against someone in authority over us. It can be a parent, a priesthood leader, a teacher, or ultimately God."[2]

Pride can blind us to our current sinful actions and, as mentioned above, make us susceptible to additional sin. It may convince us at any point to avoid or reject a necessary condition of our repentance—prematurely ending our repentance; it may even keep us from starting the repentance process altogether. Pride, then, can prevent us from being forgiven and cleansed of all our transgressions. Isaiah bid the Lord to deny forgiveness to prideful members of the house of Israel, saying, "The mean [lowly or common] man boweth not down, and the great man humbleth himself not, therefore, forgive him not" (2 Nephi 12:9).

Our pride, of course, makes it difficult to recognize the pride within us. But to repent, we need to be humble—we *must* be humble. Our spiritual growth always begins with humility. As we abandon our pride—our opposition to God's plan for us—and become "willing to submit to all things which the Lord seeth fit to inflict upon [us]" (Mosiah 3:19), we are prepared to repent and to receive the joy that comes from divine forgiveness.

DO NOT ENDEAVOR TO EXCUSE YOURSELF

Rationalizing our sins comes from pride. Rationalization is perhaps the most common method we employ to avoid full repentance and to soothe a conscience burdened with the guilt of sin. Alma warned against justifying sin when he said, "Do not endeavor to excuse yourself in the least point because of your sins" (Alma 42:30). Here are a few common excuses I have heard (followed by a brief look at some of them):

"It wasn't that bad."

"It didn't hurt anyone else."

"They'll never know."

"Everybody does it."

"They deserved it."

"It's not my fault."

"I didn't have a choice."

"I can't help it; it's just the way I am."

It wasn't that bad. We sometimes rationalize our wickedness by convincing ourselves that our sins are smaller and of less consequence than they truly are. We pretend the Lord "will justify [us] in committing a little sin; . . . and if it so be that we are guilty, [He] will beat us with a few stripes, and at last we shall be saved in the kingdom of God" (2 Nephi 28:8). But when we minimize the severity of our sins, we are, in reality, attempting to minimize or remove some of the conditions of our repentance. We are trying to tell the Lord how we will repent.

It didn't hurt anyone else. Frequently, when we trivialize our sins and their impact upon us, we also diminish in our minds the hurtful effects they have on others. We might even allow ourselves to believe that those who are unaware of our sins, including the ones we have sinned against, are unaffected. But all sins harm someone else unless they are strictly between us and the Lord. And our sins involving others will eventually be made known—either through our confession or when they "shall be spoken upon the housetops, and [our] secret acts shall be revealed" (D&C 1:3).

Our family and loved ones, even if they are not the ones we have sinned against, can be hurt by our sins we consider unimportant or insignificant. They may lose their trust and confidence in us; the family name may be tarnished. If our transgressions are indeed serious, they may affect generations. For example, our sins may destroy the testimony of our children and result in our grandchildren having little or no exposure to the gospel.

Everybody does it. We may try to downplay or obscure the significance of our transgressions by reasoning that they are global—that everyone is guilty of the same sins. But the wickedness of others does not make our sins acceptable before God or excuse our wrongdoing. William Penn, a colonial statesman and early Quaker leader, is credited with saying, "Right is right, even if everyone is against it, and wrong is wrong, even if everyone is for it."

It's not my fault. Rationalizing our sins may lead us to take the cowardly path and blame others for our transgressions. Yet, with sincere and truthful introspection, we know we are responsible for our actions; we know we are not forced to sin. Samuel the Lamanite taught, "Whosoever doeth iniquity, doeth it unto himself; for behold, ye are free; ye are permitted to act for yourselves; for behold, God . . . hath given unto you that ye might know good from evil" (Helaman 14:30–31).

If we truly do not have our agency or the proper understanding of right and wrong, we are not held accountable for our sins. Otherwise, they are ours—we own them until we repent. If we do not repent of them prior to our final judgment before the Lord, we will "be constrained to exclaim: . . . I know my guilt; I transgressed thy law, and my transgressions are mine" (2 Nephi 9:46). We will be unable to blame anyone else.

Rationalization may provide us temporary relief from the pain of transgression, but the guilt of our unrepented serious sins will continue to resurface and afflict us until we either repent or completely reject the promptings of the Spirit and silence the voice of our consciences.

Our prideful rationalizations may appear compelling and justified to us now, but they will seem foolish and indefensible when we have humbled ourselves before God or when we are compelled to be humble at the judgment bar.

YOU SEEK TO COUNSEL IN YOUR OWN WAYS

Pride may keep us from accepting the Lord's counsel given to us by His servants and through His Spirit. Jacob pleaded, "Do not say that I have spoken hard things against you; for . . . the righteous . . . love the truth" (2 Nephi 9:40). And the Lord warned, "Your sins have come up unto me, and are not pardoned, because you seek to counsel in your own ways" (D&C 56:14).

Rejecting inspired counsel is offensive to the Lord and will hinder our progress toward full repentance and forgiveness. Jacob taught, "The wise, and the learned, . . . who are puffed up because of their learning, and their wisdom, . . . they are they whom [the Lord] despiseth; and save they shall cast these things away, and consider themselves fools before God, and come down in the depths of humility, he will not open unto them" (2 Nephi 9:42).

EASILY OFFENDED

Being "puffed up" can also lead us to be easily offended. We may say to ourselves, "I have good reason to be offended by that doctrine," or "I have a right to be offended by what that member said [or did, or did not say or do]."

The Church is "the only true and living church upon the face of the whole earth" (D&C 1:30). The programs of the Church vary according to the needs of the Saints, but the doctrine and ordinances of the gospel remain constant. And while we, as members of the Church, are not perfect, "the plan of redemption, which was laid from the foundation of the world" (Alma 12:25), is perfect. Harboring offense at a particular doctrine stops our progress; removing ourselves from Church activity because we are offended puts our salvation in jeopardy.

While serving as a stake president, Elder David A. Bednar, now a member of the Quorum of the Twelve, would visit less-active members with the local bishop. Many of these members had been offended for one reason or another. After understanding the cause of their offense, Elder Bednar stated he would tell them something like the following:

Let me make sure I understand what has happened to you. Because someone at church offended you, you have not been blessed by the ordinance of the sacrament. You have withdrawn yourself from the constant companionship of the Holy Ghost. Because someone at church offended you, you have cut yourself off from priesthood ordinances and the holy temple. You have discontinued your opportunity to serve others and to learn and grow. And you are leaving barriers that will impede the spiritual progress of your children, your children's children, and the generations that will follow.

Elder Bednar and the bishop would then invite them to come back to church:

Dear friend, we are here today to counsel you that the time to stop being offended is now. Not only do we need you, but you need the blessings of the restored gospel of Jesus Christ. Please come back—now.[3]

WHO SEETH US?

We may attempt to hide our sins out of embarrassment or to avoid the consequences of our misdeeds. Concealing our sins is another manifestation of pride. When we are seeking divine mercy and relief from the debt of sin, we must fully disclose our transgressions to the Lord and, when appropriate, to others.

Isaiah warned us against thinking we can hide our sins from the Lord when he wrote, "Woe unto them that seek deep to hide their counsel from the Lord, and their works are in the dark, and they say, Who seeth us? and who knoweth us?" (Isaiah 29:15). The answer, of course, is the Lord sees and knows. In fact the Lord said, "I will show unto them . . . that I know all their works" (2 Nephi 27:27).

Jesus's conversation with the Samaritan woman at Jacob's well illustrates the Lord's knowledge of our sins:

Jesus saith unto her, Go, call thy husband, and come hither.

The woman answered and said, I have no husband. Jesus said unto her, Thou hast well said, I have no husband:

For thou hast had five husbands; and he whom thou now hast is not thy husband: in that saidst thou truly.

The woman saith unto him, Sir, I perceive that thou art a prophet. (John 4:16–19)

The Lord, at times, reveals our concealed sins to His servants. Alma and Amulek exposed Zeezrom's lies and wicked intentions through revelation. Alma told Zeezrom, "Thou hast not lied unto men only but thou hast lied unto God; for behold, he knows all thy thoughts, and thou seest that thy thoughts are made known unto us by his Spirit" (Alma 12:3).

Our serious sins need to be confessed to our bishop. We may, because of pride, be hesitant to disclose them. But when we are humble, we will confess not only our sins but also the entire gravity of our sins. We will not parcel out a little in one interview and a little more in another.

The Lord cannot bless us while we remain in our pride and hide our sins (see Proverbs 28:13; D&C 58:60). "When we undertake to cover our sins," wrote Joseph Smith, "the heavens withdraw themselves; [and] the Spirit of the Lord is grieved" (D&C 121:37).

WITH REAL INTENT

Pride keeps us from having the "mighty change in [our] hearts" (Alma 5:14) that we need to truly repent. The Lord promised, "Whosoever transgresseth against me . . . and repenteth in the sincerity of his heart, . . . I will forgive him" (Mosiah 26:29). But if we are insincere in our efforts to repent, our repentance "profiteth [us] nothing." In fact, "it is not counted unto [us] for righteousness" (Moroni 7:6–7). The Lord requires us to fulfill all the conditions of our repentance "with full purpose of heart, acting [in] no hypocrisy and no deception before God, but with real intent" (2 Nephi 31:13).

Bishop Vaughn J. Featherstone related the experience of a young man who tried at first to repent without a change of heart or real intent:

> Shortly after I had been called to the Presiding Bishopric, an Arizona stake president told me he had a young missionary candidate who needed to be interviewed for worthiness. . . .
>
> As I invited the young man into my office, after his having been cleared by his bishop and stake president, I said to him: "Apparently there has been a major transgression in your life. That's why I am involved in this interview. Would you mind being very frank and open and telling me what that transgression was?"

With head held high and in a haughty manner he responded, "There isn't *anything* I haven't done."

I responded: "Well, then, let's be more specific. Have you been involved in fornication?"

Very sarcastically, he said, "I told you I've done *everything*."

I asked, "Was it a single experience, or did it happen with more than one girl and more than once?"

And he said again, sarcastically, "Many girls and so many times I could not number them."

I said, "I would to God your transgression was not so serious."

"Well, it is," he replied.

"How about drugs?"

"I told you I've done *everything*."

Then I said, "What makes you think you're going on a mission?"

"Because I have repented," he replied. "I haven't done any of these things for a year. I know I'm going on a mission because my patriarchal blessing says I'm going on a mission. I've been ordained an elder, I've lived the way I should this past year, and I know that I'm going on a mission."

I looked at the young man sitting across the desk: twenty-one years old, laughing, sarcastic, haughty, with an attitude far removed from sincere repentance. And I said to him: "My dear young friend, I'm sorry to tell you this, but you are *not* going on a mission. Do you suppose we could send you out with your braggadocio attitude about this past life of yours, boasting of your escapades? Do you think we could send you out with the fine, clean young men who have never violated the moral code, who have kept their lives clean and pure and worthy so that they might go on missions?"

I repeated: "You're not going on a mission. In fact," I said, "you shouldn't have been ordained an elder and you really should have been tried for your membership in the Church.

"What you have committed is a series of monumental transgressions," I continued. "You haven't repented; you've just stopped doing something. Someday, after you have been to Gethsemane and back, you'll understand what true repentance is."

At this the young man started to cry. He cried for about five minutes, and during that time I didn't say a word. . . . I just sat and waited as this young man cried.

Finally he looked up and said, "I guess I haven't cried like that since I was five years old."

I told him: "If you had cried like that the first time you were tempted to violate the moral code, you may well have been going on a mission today. Now, I'm sorry, I hate to be the one to keep you from realizing your goal. I know it will be hard to go back to your friends and tell them you are not going on a mission.

"After you've been to Gethsemane," I continued, "you'll understand what I mean when I say that every person who commits a major transgression must also go to Gethsemane and back before he is forgiven."

The young man left the office, and I'm sure he wasn't very pleased; I had stood in his way and kept him from going on a mission.

About six months later, I was down in Arizona speaking at the institute at Tempe. After my talk many of the institute members came down the aisles to shake hands. As I looked up I saw this young man—the nonrepentant transgressor—coming down the aisle toward me, and at that moment the details of my interview with him came back through my mind. I recalled his braggadocio attitude, his sarcasm, his haughtiness.

I reached down to shake hands with him, and as he looked up at me I could see that something wonderful had taken place in his life. Tears streamed down his cheeks. An almost holy glow came from his countenance. I said to him, "You've been there, haven't you?"

And through tears he said, "Yes, Bishop Featherstone, I've been to Gethsemane and back."

"I know," I said. "It shows in your face. I believe now that the Lord has forgiven you."

He responded: "I'm more grateful to you than you'll ever know for not letting me go on a mission. It would have been a great disservice to me. Thanks for helping me."[4]

The Psalmist wrote, "The wicked, through the pride of his countenance, will not seek after God: God is not in all his thoughts" (Psalm 10:4). While pride prevents us from truly seeking God and repenting, humility makes us eager and gives us the strength to repent. We recognize "[our] own nothingness" (Mosiah 4:11) and view ourselves in our "own carnal state, even less than the dust of the earth" (Mosiah 4:2). Repenting, figuratively, "in sackcloth and ashes" (Mosiah 11:25)[5] testifies of our sincere desires to change and to be cleansed of all our sins.

NOTES

1. The word *pride* is always associated with sin in the scriptures. The standard works utilize other terms to describe righteous feelings of accomplishment and self-respect. For example, God expressed His satisfaction with the Creation when He said, "All things which I had made were very good" (Moses 2:31). Likewise, after Jesus was baptized of John, our Father in Heaven declared, "This is my beloved Son, in whom I am well pleased" (Matthew 3:17).

2. Ezra Taft Benson, "Beware of Pride," *Ensign*, May 1989, 4–5; emphasis in original.

3. David A. Bednar, "And Nothing Shall Offend Them," *Ensign*, November 2006, 89.

4. Vaughn J. Featherstone, *A Generation of Excellence: A Guide for Parents and Youth Leaders* (Salt Lake City: Bookcraft, 1975), 156–59; emphasis in original.

5. Sackcloth is a rough, scratchy garment made of camel or goat hair—the lowliest cloth—worn in Biblical times to demonstrate extreme humility and sorrow; repentant individuals also sprinkled or dusted themselves with ashes.

EXERCISING FAITH:
FAITH *unto* REPENTANCE

*W*HILE SCOTT AND I were exchanging some pleasantries, I was still trying to figure out how best to move beyond our casual conversation and into what we needed to discuss. He had previously told me how he had grown up in the Church, served a mission, and fulfilled his callings. Yet he had never felt the Spirit and struggled his whole life with his testimony.

I decided the best approach would be to start by telling him that I had sought for and received our Heavenly Father's guidance. "I have earnestly prayed for you and about your struggle," I began. "I feel impressed to share with you the answer I received from the Lord: You have too much pride and too little faith."

Faith and pride are incompatible with each other. Our faith grows only as we let go of our pride. Pride poisons our hearts, contaminating the soil in which we must plant and nourish our faith. In the last chapter, we discussed how pride, by appealing to the "natural man," can prevent us from repenting. But at a more fundamental level, pride can weaken or even destroy our faith—the very faith we need to repent.

FAITH IN THE LORD JESUS CHRIST

Faith is "the assurance of things hoped for, the evidence of things . . . not seen as yet" (Hebrews 11:1, 7, Joseph Smith Translation) but "which are true" (Alma 32:21). We can have faith in many things, but the only saving faith is a faith in the Lord Jesus Christ. Elder Dallin H. Oaks stated, "The first principle of the gospel is not 'faith.' The first principle of the gospel is 'Faith in the Lord Jesus Christ.'"[1]

Faith in Jesus Christ is the foundation of our repentance. We cannot repent without faith. Jesus declared to the Jews, "If ye believe not that I am [the Son of God], ye shall die in your sins" (John 8:24). The Lord made a similar statement in a revelation given through Joseph Smith but with an added explanation: "They that believe not . . . cannot be redeemed from their spiritual fall, because they repent not" (D&C 29:44).

If we do not believe in Jesus Christ or in His atoning sacrifice, to what end and purpose is our "repentance"? President Ezra Taft Benson wrote:

> Repentance means more than simply a reformation of behavior. Many men and women in the world demonstrate great willpower and self-discipline in overcoming bad habits and the weaknesses of the flesh. Yet at the same time they give no thought to the Master, sometimes even openly rejecting Him. Such changes of behavior, even if in a positive direction, do not constitute true repentance.[2]

WHEN FAITH IS WANTING

Joseph Smith taught that when "faith is wanting, the fruits are [wanting],"[3] and where faith is weak people will "grow weary in their minds, and the adversary will have power over them and destroy them."[4]

I have met with several members who tried but initially failed to repent of their sins. Their faith was weak, and they had placed repentance, the second principle of the gospel, before faith. But after strengthening their faith in Jesus Christ, they were able to repent of their sins and receive forgiveness from the Lord. Amulek clearly and beautifully testified of this important truth, saying,

> He that exercises no faith unto repentance is exposed to the whole law of the demands of justice; therefore only unto him that has faith unto repentance is brought about the great and eternal plan of redemption. (Alma 34:16)

If you are discouraged or perhaps feel that you are beyond redemption and will never be worthy of celestial glory, remember, God doesn't feel that way. With faith in the Lord Jesus Christ you can repent and be forgiven. Professor and author Stephen E. Robinson made this insightful observation:

> Not only must we believe that [Jesus] is who he says he is, we must also believe that he can do what he says he can do. We must not only believe *in* Christ, we must also *believe Christ* when he says he can clean us up and make us celestial.[5]

If we are questioning whether or not the Lord will honor His promise to bless us for keeping His commandments or if we think a particular commandment is too difficult to obey, our doubts are manifestations of our lack of faith. If we repeat the same sin again and again, our faith is not yet strong enough to sustain us.

We can, with greater faith, overcome our sins. The Lord said, "If ye will have faith in me ye shall have power to do whatsoever thing is expedient in me" (Moroni 7:33). Indeed, we can "withstand every temptation of the devil, with [our] faith on the Lord Jesus Christ" (Alma 37:33).

With faith we can pay tithing and know the Lord will fulfill His promise to abundantly bless us for our obedience. With faith we can keep the law of chastity and honor the sacred powers of procreation within the bonds of marriage. And with faith we can obey the Word of Wisdom and respect our bodies as temples of God. With faith comes obedience, and obedience builds faith.

A SAVING FAITH

How do we obtain or develop a saving faith—a faith Joseph Smith described as "in God unto life and salvation"?[6] Below are three key elements.

Understanding the True Nature of God

We must learn about God and His existence from those who know the truth about Him—His prophets and apostles. When we read the scriptures and attend church, we will learn that God is loving, forgiving, and full of compassion; that He will not lie to us, change the conditions of our repentance, or alter what we must do to gain salvation. When we have acquired these important truths about God's character, we can begin to exercise faith in Him.[7] Many of the Lamanites gained a saving faith after they were taught the gospel of Jesus Christ and understood the true nature of God:

> Salvation hath come unto [the Lamanites] through the preaching of the Nephites; and . . . [they] are brought to the knowledge of the truth, and . . . are led to believe the holy scriptures, yea, the prophecies of the holy prophets, which are written, which leadeth them to faith on the Lord, and unto repentance. (Helaman 15:4, 7)

Desiring to Believe

If we "desire to believe" and do not "resist the Spirit of the Lord" (Alma 32:27–28), the Holy Ghost will confirm gospel truths to our souls—both while we are studying "the doctrine of Christ" (2 Nephi 31:21) and in answer to our sincere prayers. But if we do not allow the Lord's words to be "planted in [our] heart[s]" (Alma 32:28), we become like "many of the rising generation" (Mosiah 26:1) in the days of King Mosiah:

> And now because of their unbelief they could not understand the word of God; and their hearts were hardened. And they . . . remained . . . in their carnal and sinful state; for they would not call upon the Lord their God. (Mosiah 26:3–4)

Obeying the Commandments

We can fortify our budding faith by walking "circumspectly before God" and by obeying "his commandments and his statutes" (Helaman 15:5). As we keep the commandments, we start to notice God blessing us for our obedience, and our faith immediately grows. We begin to have, as Joseph Smith stated, "an actual knowledge that the course [we] are pursuing is according to the will of God."[8]

As we increase our faith, the Lord will "make weak things become strong unto [us]" (Ether 12:27). We will find it easier to repent of our sins and to keep the commandments. In fact, we will gain the desire and the ability to "obey . . . with exactness" (Alma 57:21).

One day our faith will be fully rewarded. We will have a "perfect knowledge of God" (Ether 3:20) and "faith no longer" (Ether 3:19), for we will be redeemed from the Fall and brought back to live in His presence.

FAITH LEADS TO HOPE

In addition to repentance, our faith also gives us hope—hope that we will be clean again and worthy to gain "a place at the right hand of God" (Ether 12:4). Mormon explained the relationship between faith and hope:

> How is it that ye can attain unto faith, save ye shall have hope? And what is it that ye shall hope for? Behold I say unto you that ye shall have hope through the atonement of Christ and the power of his resurrection, to be raised unto life eternal, and this because of your faith in him according to the promise. Wherefore, if a man have faith he must needs have hope; for without faith there cannot be any hope. (Moroni 7:40–42)

We must never allow Satan to rob us of hope—he knows we will lose hope if we continue to sin (see Moroni 10:22). Our salvation depends on us keeping our faith and hope alive.

I have seen Satan open "the gates of hell" (3 Nephi 11:39) and besiege individuals with numerous temptations immediately after they confessed their sins and vowed never to repeat them. Some of the temptations came in new and unexpected ways—even novel ways. If the errant members were not keenly aware of Satan's relentless desire for their failure or prepared for his onslaught, they would frequently succumb to temptation again. Their feelings of discouragement and hopelessness would immediately return with greater intensity than they had felt before. In their despair they would tell me, "I feel I'm the only one who cannot overcome his sins. There's no hope for me."

But there is hope! With faith in Jesus Christ and in His atoning sacrifice, we can receive the power to repent and have "a perfect brightness of hope" (2 Nephi 31:20).

THY FAITH HATH MADE THEE WHOLE

After Enos prayed all day long and into the night for forgiveness of his sins, a voice came unto him and said, "Enos, thy sins are forgiven thee, and thou shalt be blessed." Enos asked, "Lord, how is it done?" The Lord replied, "Because of thy faith in Christ; . . . wherefore, go to, thy faith hath made thee whole" (Enos 1:5, 7–8).

Luke wrote of a sinful woman who was also forgiven because of her faith. She had humbly approached Jesus while He was dining with a Pharisee named Simon:

> And, behold, a woman in the city, which was a sinner, when she knew that Jesus sat at meat in the Pharisee's house, brought an alabaster box of ointment, and stood at his feet behind him weeping, and began to wash his feet with tears, and did wipe them with the hairs of her head, and kissed his feet, and anointed them with the ointment.
>
> Now when the Pharisee which had bidden him saw it, he spake within himself, saying, This man, if he were a prophet, would have known who and what manner of woman this is that toucheth him: for she is a sinner.
>
> And Jesus answering said unto him, Simon, I have somewhat to say unto thee. And he saith, Master, say on.
>
> There was a certain creditor which had two debtors: the one owed five hundred pence, and the other fifty. And when they had nothing to pay, he frankly forgave them both. Tell me therefore, which of them will love him most?
>
> Simon answered and said, I suppose that he, to whom he forgave most. And he said unto him, Thou hast rightly judged.
>
> And he turned to the woman, and said unto Simon, Seest thou this woman? I entered into thine house, thou gavest me no water for my feet: but she hath washed my feet with tears, and wiped them with the hairs of her head. Thou gavest me no kiss: but this woman since the time I came in hath not ceased to kiss my feet. My head with oil thou didst not anoint: but this woman hath anointed my feet with ointment. Wherefore I say unto thee, Her sins, which are many, are forgiven; for she loved much: but to whom little is forgiven, the same loveth little.
>
> And he said unto her, *Thy sins are forgiven. . . . Thy faith hath saved thee; go in peace.* (Luke 7:37–48, 50; emphasis added)

Our faith can save us. After we fulfill all the conditions of our repentance, we will receive the same blessings that were given to King Benjamin's people: "The Spirit of the Lord came upon them, and they were filled with joy, having received a remission of their sins, and having peace of conscience, *because of the exceeding faith which they had in Jesus Christ*" (Mosiah 4:3; emphasis added).

NOTES

1. Dallin H. Oaks, "'Faith in the Lord Jesus Christ,'" *Ensign*, May 1994, 98.

2. Ezra Taft Benson, "A Mighty Change of Heart," *Ensign*, October 1989, 2.

3. Joseph Smith, *History of the Church of Jesus Christ of Latter-day Saints* (Salt Lake City: The Church of Jesus Christ of Latter-day Saints, 1949), 5:218.

4. Joseph Smith, *Lectures on Faith* (Salt Lake City: Deseret Book, 1985), 71.

5. Stephen E. Robinson, *Believing Christ: The Parable of the Bicycle and Other Good News* (Salt Lake City: Deseret Book, 1992), 10; emphasis in original.

6. Smith, *Lectures on Faith*, 38.

7. See Ibid., 38–48.

8. Ibid., 67–68.

GAINING AWARENESS: *I* ACKNOWLEDGE *My* TRANSGRESSIONS

*T*HE LORD "CALLETH upon all men, and he commandeth all men everywhere to repent." He declared: "Hearken and hear, O ye inhabitants of the earth. Listen . . . and hear [my] voice" (D&C 133:16). When we listen to the Lord's voice and hear His command to repent, we become aware of our sins. This new knowledge and awareness—the recognition of our sins—enables us to choose repentance over wickedness and, when coupled with faith and humility, makes our repentance possible.

In a revelation given through Joseph Smith, the Lord enumerated some of the many ways He calls us to repentance:

> How oft have I called upon you by the mouth of my servants, and by the ministering of angels, and by mine own voice, and by the voice of thunderings, and by the voice of lightnings, and by the voice of tempests, and by the voice of earthquakes, and great hailstorms, and by the voice of famines and pestilences of every kind, and by the great sound of a trump, and by the voice of judgment, and by the voice of mercy all the day long, and by the voice of glory and honor and the riches of eternal life. (D&C 43:25)

The Lord calls to us with promises of mercy and blessings or, when necessary, with warnings of consequences and judgments. In this chapter we will review some of the methods He uses to help us hear His voice and recognize our sins.

THE LIGHT OF CHRIST

Each of us has been given the Light or Spirit of Christ, a conscience, to guide us in making righteous choices. Mormon wrote,

> The Spirit of Christ is given to every man, that he may know good from evil; wherefore, I show unto you the way to judge; for every thing which inviteth to do good, and to persuade to believe in Christ, is sent forth by the power and gift of Christ; . . . But whatsoever thing persuadeth men to do evil, and believe not in Christ, . . . is of the devil; . . . Wherefore, . . . search diligently in the light of Christ that ye may know good from evil. (Moroni 7:16–17, 19)

If we are thinking about committing a sin or when we have broken a commandment of God, we will be "convicted by [our] own conscience" (John 8:9). Our consciences, however, can be silenced— "seared with a hot iron" (1 Timothy 4:2)—if we continually choose to be disobedient.

THE HOLY GHOST

As members of the Church, we "were baptized with fire and with the Holy Ghost" (3 Nephi 9:20). We were given the right to the constant companionship of the third member of the Godhead to guide us in our daily lives.

The Holy Ghost is a much greater gift than the Light of Christ. Our consciences help us to distinguish right from wrong whereas the Holy Ghost "beareth record of the Father and the Son" (Moses 5:9). He testifies to us of the Atonement of Jesus Christ and teaches us "the truth of all things" (Moroni 10:5).

Jacob taught, "The Spirit speaketh the truth and lieth not. Wherefore, it speaketh . . . for the salvation of our souls" (Jacob 4:13). Sometimes the truth we need to hear—the knowledge we need for our salvation—is that we need to repent.

The Holy Ghost speaks to us most often when we pray, study the scriptures, and worship at church—when we are prepared to listen and to learn. But He may also inspire us to repent or warn us about sin at any time.

For example, I met with an active member who had put himself in a difficult situation after he ignored the promptings of the Spirit. He had developed a good working relationship with one of his coworkers, and because of their friendship, she confided in him that she was unhappy in her marriage. He listened sympathetically as she criticized her husband and shared her marital problems. He told himself he could help her by offering her sound advice based on gospel principles. But as they talked about her marriage, he would often feel the Spirit whisper, "You shouldn't be doing this." Soon their conversations were no longer just at work but continued at lunch or over dinner. And despite his growing emotional relationship with her, he continued to ignore the Spirit's constant warnings. Only after she told him she loved him did he finally recognize the seriousness of his mistake.

THE WORDS OF CHRIST

Alma taught his son Helaman that "the word[s] of Christ . . . will point to you a straight course to eternal bliss" (Alma 37:44) and counseled him, saying: "O my son, do not let us be slothful because of the easiness of the way; for . . . if we will look [read the scriptures] we may live forever" (Alma 37:46).

If we wish to remain spiritually strong and to resist temptation, we need to immerse ourselves in the scriptures every day. They will teach us "all things what [we] should do" (2 Nephi 32:3)—and what we shouldn't do. Mormon testified of the great power the scriptures have in helping us discern right from wrong:

> Yea, we see that whosoever will may lay hold upon the word of God, which is quick and powerful, which shall divide asunder all the cunning and the snares and the wiles of the devil, and lead the man of Christ in a strait and narrow course across that everlasting gulf of misery which is prepared to engulf the wicked—and land their souls, yea, their immortal souls, at the right hand of God in the kingdom of heaven. (Helaman 3:29–30)

I SEND UNTO YOU PROPHETS AND WISE MEN

The Lord sends us "prophets, and wise men" (Matthew 23:34) to help us recognize our sins. We can hear those whom He has sent by consistently attending sacrament and other Church meetings and by receiving counsel from Church leaders in general conference. Mormon observed:

> The preaching of the word [of God] had a great tendency to lead the people to do that which was just—yea, it had had more powerful effect upon the minds of the people than the sword, or anything else. (Alma 31:5)

For instance, after Peter taught and testified of Jesus Christ on the day of Pentecost, many of the multitude were "pricked in their heart[s]" and asked Peter, "What shall we do?" He answered, saying, "Repent, and be baptized every one of you in the name of Jesus Christ for the remission of sins" (Acts 2:37–38).

THE RIGHTEOUS EXAMPLES OF OTHERS

By carefully observing the righteous examples of others, we will recognize not only virtues in their lives we should develop but also sins in our lives we should abandon. Here are two examples.

Emma, a member of our ward, was being treated for cancer. Whenever I entered her hospital room for a visit after first donning gloves, a gown, and a mask, she would cheerfully say, "Hi, Bishop! Thanks for coming to see me!" She was always positive and upbeat. All of us who went to comfort her felt that we were the ones being comforted. She held no grudge against God for her trials; she only wanted to endure them well. The cancer eventually took her life, but she never faltered in her attitude and testimony. She instilled in us a desire to always be grateful and to have greater faith in our Heavenly Father's plan for us.

King Lamoni, king over the land of Ishmael, believed in a "Great Spirit," but he also believed there was no sin and that "whatsoever [he] did was right" (Alma 18:5). He had killed many of his servants because they had failed to guard his flocks against marauding thieves. However, after he was told of "the faithfulness of Ammon in preserving his flocks" (Alma 18:2) and of the miraculous manner by which Ammon protected them, King Lamoni "began to fear exceedingly . . . lest he had done wrong in slaying his servants" (Alma 18:5). He thought Ammon was the Great Spirit and had come to punish him for his transgressions. Ammon's example awakened in King Lamoni a recognition of his sins and prepared him to be taught the plan of redemption.

The scriptures contain many other examples of faithful and obedient men and women—all worthy of emulation. We can also follow the examples of righteous individuals the Lord places in our path every day. Their good works will help us recognize our sinful actions and motivate us to repent. And above all, our Savior's love and perfect life provide a pattern for our lives.

THE CHASTENING HAND OF THE LORD

"Now is the time for you to repent! Your soul is in jeopardy!" The Spirit has prompted me to issue this forceful warning to only two or three individuals. They had confessed their serious sins but, being full of pride, felt little remorse and no desire to change. They expected their confessions would be the only condition of repentance required of them, and they thought, as did Corianton, that it was unjust for a sinner to be punished (see Alma 42:1).

We are subject to divine chastening when we ignore the gentler invitations from the Lord to repent. Unlike the loving, hopeful encouragement God gives to humble sinners, He chastens prideful transgressors:

Except the Lord doth chasten his people with many afflictions, . . . they will not remember him. . . . They do not desire that the Lord their God . . . should rule and reign over them; . . . they do set at naught his counsels, and they will not that he should be their guide. (Helaman 12:3, 6)

The Israelites "spake against God, and against Moses" (Numbers 21:5) after they were freed from Egypt—complaining about their trials and living conditions. Displeased with their murmuring and wickedness, the Lord "sent fiery serpents among the people, and they bit the people; and much people of Israel died" (Numbers 21:6). The chastened Israelites said to Moses,

We have sinned, for we have spoken against the Lord, and against thee; pray unto the Lord, that he take away the serpents from us. And Moses prayed for the people.

And the Lord said unto Moses, Make thee a fiery serpent, and set it upon a pole: and it shall come to pass, that every one that is bitten, when he looketh upon it, shall live.

And Moses made a serpent of brass, and put it upon a pole, and it came to pass, that if a serpent had bitten any man, when he beheld the serpent of brass, he lived. (Numbers 21:7–9)

Not all our trials, however, constitute a call to repentance, so it is important that we recognize the source of our adversities. Some of our hardships in life are administered by God and provide a means for our sanctification; others are consequences resulting from our unrighteous choices. But many of our trials come from our carelessness or poor judgment, the sinful or inadvertent acts of others, or simply because we live in a fallen, telestial world. After the tower of Siloam fell and killed eighteen people, Jesus asked, referring to those who perished, "Think ye that they were sinners above all men that dwelt in Jerusalem? I tell you, Nay" (Luke 13:4–5). Joseph Smith taught,

Many of the righteous shall fall a prey to disease, to pestilence, etc., by reason of the weakness of the flesh. . . . So . . . it is an unhallowed principle to say that [they] have transgressed because they have been preyed upon by disease or death.[1]

"No chastening for the present seemeth to be joyous, but grievous," observed Paul, "nevertheless afterward it yieldeth the peaceable fruit of righteousness unto them which are exercised thereby" (Hebrews 12:11). God's chastisement is for our benefit. When we recognize and accept the chastening hand of the Lord, we are led to repentance. I received the following letter from a humbled member that illustrates this principle:

Although it is a hard lesson to learn, I know that sometimes it takes "a slap in the face" for us to open our eyes and come unto the Lord. My eyes are wide open! . . . I can't wait to complete the repentance process. I know it might be a long process, but I am more than willing to [do what it takes].[2]

THE SPIRIT OF THE LAW

Recognizing our sins means we acknowledge our violations of both the letter and the spirit of the law. Unlike the rigid and literal compliance expected of the Israelites under the law of Moses, the law of the gospel requires us to obey the commandments with a willing heart and a genuine love of God and all mankind. In the Sermon on the Mount, for example, Jesus taught that the inward and invisible feelings of anger and lust are sins—just like the much more serious outward and visible actions of murder and adultery:

> Ye have heard that it was said by them of old time, Thou shalt not kill; . . . But I say unto you, That whosoever is angry with his brother without a cause shall be in danger of the judgment. . . .
>
> Ye have heard that it was said by them of old time, Thou shalt not commit adultery: But I say unto you, That whosoever looketh on a woman to lust after her hath committed adultery with her already in his heart. (Matthew 5:21–22, 27–28)

Our salvation depends on our ability to hear and to answer God's call to repentance. The Lord warned Joseph Smith, "Because of transgression, if thou art not aware thou wilt fall" (D&C 3:9). Amulek, because of his pride, refused to listen to the voice of the Lord until he was visited by an angel. He said:

> I did harden my heart, for I was called many times and I would not hear; therefore I knew concerning these things, yet I would not know; therefore I went on rebelling against God, in the wickedness of my heart. (Alma 10:6)

We will hear His voice when we are humble. And in faith we can respond with an honest desire to overcome our sins: "I acknowledge my transgressions" (Psalm 51:3), and "I will repent [and] return to my God" (Alma 34:34).

NOTES

1. Joseph Smith, *History of the Church of Jesus Christ of Latter-day Saints* (Salt Lake City: The Church of Jesus Christ of Latter-day Saints, 1949), 4:11.
2. Personal correspondence.

OFFERING PRAYER:
CRY MIGHTILY *to the* LORD

*W*HEN WE SIN, particularly if it is a serious sin, we may feel unworthy or too ashamed to pray. Satan will try to convince us to stop praying and to hide from our Father in Heaven, "for the evil spirit teacheth not a man to pray, but teacheth him that he must not pray" (2 Nephi 32:8). Yet the Lord, who loves us and is already aware of all our sins, wants us to continue to "pray without ceasing" (Mosiah 26:39). The times we feel the least like praying are the times we probably need to pray the most. Brigham Young taught, "If we do not feel like it, we should pray till we *do*."[1]

Although our Father in Heaven hears our prayers, He may be slow to answer them if we continue in sin or fail to repent. The Lord, referring to the people of King Noah, told the prophet Abinadi, "Except they repent in sackcloth and ashes, and cry mightily to the Lord their God, I will not hear [answer] their prayers" (Mosiah 11:25). Similarly, God delayed answering the prayers of the early Saints in Missouri because of their transgressions:

> They were slow to hearken unto the voice of the Lord their God; therefore, the Lord their God is slow to hearken unto their prayers, to answer them in the day of their trouble. In the day of their peace they esteemed lightly my counsel; but, in the day of their trouble, of necessity they feel after me. (D&C 101:7–8)

If you do not feel the Spirit when you pray or if it seems like the heavens are far away, don't give up. Keep praying fervently and frequently. Prayer is a condition of our repentance. When we pray we are able to exercise faith, demonstrate humility, confess our sins to the Lord, seek His help, and ask His forgiveness.

Alma the Elder's prayers were not immediately answered while he was repenting of his iniquities. But the answers eventually came— and so will ours. He told the members of the Church,

> I . . . did many things which were abominable in the sight of the Lord, which caused me sore repentance; nevertheless, after much tribulation, the Lord did hear my cries, and did answer my prayers. (Mosiah 23:9–10)

After we have fulfilled all the conditions of our repentance, the Lord will answer our pleas for forgiveness, and He will say to us, "Thy sins are forgiven thee, according to thy petition, for thy prayers . . . have come up into my ears" (D&C 90:1).

And with forgiveness comes a greater measure of the Spirit. Through the Spirit we will receive guidance and direction in our prayers. The Lord said, "He that asketh in the Spirit asketh according to the will of God; wherefore it is done even as he asketh" (D&C 46:30). Indeed, after we "are purified and cleansed from all sin, [we] shall ask whatsoever [we] will in the name of Jesus and it shall be done" (D&C 50:29).

WHAT LACK I YET?

We cannot repent if we do not see ourselves as we really are—if we are blind to our transgressions. As we seek to be more like our Heavenly Father, we will naturally want to recognize our sins and remove them from our lives. For example, Joseph Smith prayed for forgiveness and to know if he was accepted of the Lord:

> I betook myself to prayer and supplication to Almighty God for forgiveness of all my sins and follies, and also for a manifestation to me, that I might know of my state and standing before him. (Joseph Smith—History 1:29)

The Lord knows us perfectly, and He knows what we need to repent of. "Repent, therefore, of those things which are not pleasing in my sight, saith the Lord, for *the Lord will show them unto you*" (D&C 66:3; emphasis added). When we ask God to show us our transgressions, He will reveal to us our unrighteous thoughts, words, and actions that we never previously considered to be sinful.

Before we ask, however, we need to prepare our hearts "to receive and obey the instructions" (D&C 132:3) we will be given. A rich young man asked Jesus, "What good thing shall I do, that I may have eternal life?" (Matthew 19:16). Jesus answered him by specifying some of the Ten Commandments and citing the second great commandment—to love our neighbor as ourselves. "All these things have I kept from my youth up," affirmed the young man. And in a sincere desire to know if there was anything further he needed to do, he asked this important question, "What lack I yet?" Jesus replied, "If thou wilt be perfect, go and sell that thou hast, and give to the poor, . . . and come and follow me." The young man was unprepared to obey these commandments from the Lord, and "he went away sorrowful" (Matthew 19:20–22).

PRAY WITH REAL INTENT

If we think we are too weak and not ready to repent of our sins quite yet, praying for forgiveness may be premature. Mormon taught it is "counted evil unto a man, if he shall pray and not with real intent of heart; yea, and it profiteth him nothing" (Moroni 7:9). This does not mean we should not pray. We can still pray for humility, a change of heart, additional faith, or the strength to overcome the stumbling block that is preventing us from repenting. We can pray for the *desire* to repent and to keep the commandments—for the desire "to be a greater follower of righteousness" (Abraham 1:2).

THE PRAYERS OF THE RIGHTEOUS

Paul wrote that his "heart's desire and prayer to God for Israel" (Romans 10:1) was that they might be saved, for they had "not submitted themselves unto the righteousness of God" (Romans 10:3). The Lord has commanded us to pray for others, and He answers our prayers according to our faith and His wisdom. The wicked people of

Ammonihah were spared destruction because of "the prayers of the righteous" (Alma 10:23).[2] And Alma the Younger, when he was "a very wicked and an idolatrous man" (Mosiah 27:8), received a visit from an angel because of the faith-filled prayers of his father and many members of the Church. The angel told Alma,

> Thy father . . . has prayed with much faith concerning thee that thou mightest be brought to the knowledge of the truth; therefore, for this purpose have I come to convince thee of the power and authority of God, that the prayers of his servants might be answered according to their faith. (Mosiah 27:14)

If we are struggling in sin, it is appropriate to ask others to pray for us that we will have the faith and the strength to overcome our sins (without necessarily revealing to them the nature of our transgressions). We should likewise pray for others in need—individually and by name. James counseled us: "Pray one for another. . . . The effectual fervent prayer of a righteous man availeth much" (James 5:16).

FASTING AND PRAYER

Never underestimate the combined power of fasting and prayer—together they can help us conquer our sins. Fasting can "loose the bands of wickedness, . . . undo the heavy burdens, and . . . break every yoke" (Isaiah 58:6). Many of the Nephites, for example, "did fast and pray oft," which led them to greater faith and "to the purifying and the sanctification of their hearts" (Helaman 3:35). Fasting and prayer can likewise strengthen our faith and increase our ability to purge our hearts of every sinful desire.

SUFFER US NOT TO BE LED INTO TEMPTATION

The Lord's Prayer, which is a model for our prayers, includes a petition to our Father in Heaven to "suffer us not to be led into temptation" (Matthew 6:14, Joseph Smith Translation). The Lord wants us to ask Him for help in avoiding temptation. In addition, God warns us many times in the scriptures to "pray always lest ye enter into temptation" (3 Nephi 18:18) and to "pray always . . . that you may conquer Satan" (D&C 10:5). When we pray to resist evil and keep a prayer continually in our hearts, God will protect and deliver us from Satan. We will be rescued from "the power of some actual being from the unseen world"—just as Joseph Smith was rescued immediately before he received the First Vision—when we use all our "powers to call upon God to deliver [us]" (Joseph Smith—History 1:16).

NOTES

1. Brigham Young, in *Journal of Discourses* (London: Latter-day Saints' Book Depot, 1871), 13:155; emphasis in original.
2. However, after all the righteous citizens were either killed or banished from the city, "the people of Ammonihah were destroyed; yea, every living soul" (Alma 16:9).

FEELING SORROW: *Godly* SORROW *Worketh* REPENTANCE

A WAVE OF SORROW immediately sweeps over us after we recognize our sins. We are awakened "to a lively sense" of our wickedness, and our souls are filled "with guilt, and pain, and anguish" (Mosiah 2:38). Alma explained the reason for our sorrow:

> Now, how could a man repent except he should sin? How could he sin if there was no law? How could there be a law save there was a punishment? Now, *there was a punishment affixed,* and a just law given, *which brought remorse of conscience* unto man. (Alma 42:17–18; emphasis added)

Remorse certainly comes from knowing our sinful actions can have bitter consequences and bring upon us the punishments of God—including losing blessings, experiencing the mental pain of guilt, and feeling unclean. But the true nature of our sorrow depends on the level of our faith and the amount of love we have for God. Paul, in his second letter to the Corinthians, wrote,

> Now I rejoice, not that ye were made sorry, but that ye sorrowed to repentance: for ye were made sorry after a godly manner. . . . For godly sorrow worketh repentance to salvation . . . but the sorrow of the world worketh death. (2 Corinthians 7:9–10)

GODLY SORROW

What is godly sorrow? It is profound sadness for "offend[ing] God" when we "obey[ed] not his commandments" (D&C 59:21) and an overwhelming desire to be found again in His favor. It is anguish in knowing we added to Christ's incomprehensible agony in the Garden of Gethsemane—a suffering so "sore," "exquisite," and "hard to bear" (D&C 19:15) that it caused Him "to tremble because of pain, and to bleed at every pore, and to suffer both body and spirit" (D&C 19:18).[1]

Godly sorrow is to be bitterly disappointed we allowed ourselves to succumb to temptation; we despair we were vulnerable to one of the "the fiery darts of the adversary" (1 Nephi 15:24) and failed to "conquer Satan" (D&C 10:5). We are angry at ourselves for needlessly stepping into the path of temptation or for turning a blind eye to the devil's cunning. We detest our sinful actions, knowing our disobedience was primarily selfish in nature and lacking in "love towards God and all men" (Mosiah 2:4).

Godly sorrow makes us anxious to repair any hurt or damage we did to others, and we are willing to submit to whatever the Lord and His servants require of us to be forgiven and to be clean again. Even if our sins are only between us and the Lord, our desire to repent is no less urgent.

With godly sorrow we have "a broken heart and a contrite spirit" (2 Nephi 2:7) and our "sins trouble [us], with that trouble which shall bring [us] down unto repentance" (Alma 42:29). Thus, as Elder Marion D. Hanks stated, godly sorrow is "purposeful, constructive, [and] cleansing."[2]

WORLDLY SORROW

Worldly sorrow, on the other hand, is sorrow "not unto repentance" but "the sorrowing of the damned, because the Lord would not always suffer them to take happiness in sin" (Mormon 2:13).

We are disappointed, perhaps even angered, when we are caught doing something wrong or our concealed action is exposed. We are frustrated when we are prevented from continuing in our sinful ways. We resent having to pay the penalties or endure the consequences of our transgressions.

With worldly sorrow we have no true remorse for breaking divine laws, no hatred of sin, and no shame before God for committing sin. "Were they ashamed when they had committed abomination?" the Lord asked of Jerusalem. "Nay," said the Lord in answer to His own question, "they were not at all ashamed, neither could they blush" (Jeremiah 6:15). The only shame we have comes from our wounded pride.

Worldly sorrow has little redeeming value and provides no eternal progression. Although we may abandon our sins because of the accompanying punishments or consequences, there is no true reformation or desire to change—only a desire to have our punishments removed and perhaps a longing to return to our sinful ways. We do "not come unto Jesus with broken hearts and contrite spirits" (Mormon 2:14), nor do we come unto the Savior for forgiveness. Worldly sorrow, then, is sorrow that "worketh [spiritual] death" (2 Corinthians 7:10).

ANGUISH OF SOUL

We have all felt "bitter pain and anguish of soul" (Alma 38:8) after humbly recognizing our sins. On several occasions members have called me immediately after committing a sin. The conversations were often very similar. The remorseful transgressor, in a trembling, anxious voice, would say, "Hi, Bishop. I've made a terrible mistake. I've committed a serious sin. Can I come and talk with you?" After expressing my gratitude to them for calling, I would ask, "When would you like to meet?" And invariably the answer was, "Can we meet right now or very soon? I can't believe I did what I did. It's horrible. I'm terrified. I don't know what will happen to me [usually referring to their Church membership status]. I deserve the harshest punishment. I feel so dirty, so unclean. I'm afraid I can never be forgiven. I've let myself and everyone else down. I'm so very sorry."

Feelings of remorse are a necessary and useful condition of our repentance, for they can bring us back to righteousness. After Martin Harris confirmed to Joseph Smith that he had lost the first 116 pages of the Book of Mormon, Joseph was immediately overcome with intense sorrow. He cried out:

> Oh! Martin, have you lost that manuscript? Have you broken your oath [to show the manuscript to only certain individuals]

and brought down condemnation upon my head as well as your own? . . .

All is lost, is lost! What shall I do? I have sinned. It is I who tempted the wrath of God by asking him for that which I had no right to ask. . . . And how shall I appear before the Lord? Of what rebuke am I not worthy from the angel of the Most High?[3]

Lucy Mack Smith, Joseph's mother, described how Joseph "wept and groaned, and walk[ed] the floor continually."[4] The whole family was affected:

Our sobs and groans and the most bitter lamentations filled the house. Joseph, in particular, was more distressed than the rest, for he knew definitely and by sorrowful experience the consequence of what would seem to others to be a very trifling neglect of duty. He continued walking backwards and forwards, weeping and grieving.[5]

Joseph's godly sorrow led to full repentance:

I commenced humbling myself in mighty prayer before the Lord, and as I poured out my soul in supplication to him, that if possible I might obtain mercy at his hands and be forgiven of all that I had done which was contrary to his will, an angel stood before me and answered me, saying, that I had sinned in delivering the manuscript into the hands of a wicked man, and as I had ventured to become responsible for this man's faithfulness, I would of necessity suffer the consequences of his indiscretion, and I must now give back the Urim and Thummim [used to translate the Book of Mormon] into his (the angel's) hands.

This I did as I was directed, and as I handed them to him he remarked, "If you are very humble and penitent, it may be you will receive them again."[6]

After two to three months of "supplications to God, without cessation,"[7] Joseph was forgiven:

The angel was rejoiced when he gave me back the Urim and Thummim, and he told me that the Lord was pleased with my faithfulness and humility, and loved me for my penitence and diligence in prayer.[8]

SORROW AND CLINICAL DEPRESSION

Our anguish of soul can be a very real and oppressive feeling. Zeezrom, after being exposed trying to falsely accuse Alma and Amulek of crimes punishable by prison or death, "began to tremble under a consciousness of his guilt" (Alma 12:1). He declared to the people, "I am guilty, and these men are spotless before God" (Alma 14:7). Many days later, the scriptures record,

> Zeezrom lay sick . . . with a burning fever . . . caused by the great tribulations of his mind on account of his wickedness. . . . And [his sins] did harrow up his mind until it did become exceedingly sore, having no deliverance; therefore he began to be scorched with a burning heat. (Alma 15:3)

Although sin, as in Zeezrom's case, can cause extreme mental anguish and most certainly depress our spirits, clinical depression experienced by many individuals is usually not the result of sin. Feelings of worthlessness and excessive guilt are common symptoms of depression. Many who suffer from depression continue to needlessly criticize themselves over the smallest of sins and weaknesses or repeatedly feel guilt and anguish for sins long since forgiven. Some feel the Lord is punishing them with depression to get them to repent with greater humility and sorrow, or they search their souls in vain trying to find the sin responsible for their depression when the actual cause has nothing to do with sin.

If you are feeling depressed, you should consider consulting with your bishop or a mental health professional to determine if your depression is the result of feeling sorrow for wickedness or a mood disorder brought on by other causes (such as heredity, neurochemical changes, or environmental factors).

BY THE THINGS WHICH THEY SUFFER

Along with feeling sorrow, we will also suffer some amount of punishment for our sins. For example, the laws established by King Mosiah and recognized by the people in the reign of the judges were "put in force upon all those who did transgress [them]"—each lawbreaker "suffering according to that which he had done." By enforcing the laws, the people "became more still, and durst not commit any wickedness" (Alma 1:32–33).

The same principle applies to spiritual laws. The Lord said, "My people must needs be chastened until they learn obedience, if it must needs be, by the things which they suffer" (D&C 105:6).

Sin always brings sorrow and suffering. While the amount and timing will vary individually, we cannot escape God's punishments completely. Even when we repent we must still endure some sorrow and suffering while we are repenting, for they help change our hearts and motivate us to forever abandon our sins. Elder Dallin H. Oaks stated,

> The unrepentant transgressor must suffer for his own sins. . . . The person who repents does not need to suffer "even as" the Savior suffered for that sin. Sinners who are repenting will experience some suffering, but because of their repentance and the Atonement, they will not experience the full, "exquisite" extent of eternal torment the Savior suffered.[9]

In his psalm Nephi wrote, "My heart exclaimeth: O wretched man that I am! Yea, my heart sorroweth because of my flesh; my soul grieveth because of mine iniquities" (2 Nephi 4:17). Thankfully, repentance and the Atonement of Jesus Christ permanently remove all the guilt, pain, and anguish of sin. And it is godly sorrow, as Nephi felt, that brings us to repentance and to eternal life, for only "the truly penitent are saved" (Alma 42:24).

NOTES

1. See Ezra Taft Benson, "A Mighty Change of Heart," *Ensign*, October 1989, 4.
2. Marion D. Hanks, "He Means Me," *Ensign*, May 1979, 76.
3. Lucy Mack Smith, *The Revised and Enhanced History of Joseph Smith By His Mother*, ed. Scot Facer Proctor and Maurine Jensen Proctor (Salt Lake City: Bookcraft, 1996), 165–66.
4. Ibid., 166.
5. Ibid.

6. Ibid., 173–74.
7. Ibid., 176.
8. Ibid.
9. Dallin H. Oaks, "Sin and Suffering," *Ensign*, July 1992, 72.

MAKING CONFESSION: I *Will* DECLARE *Mine* INIQUITY

OUR PROGRESS IN completing some of the conditions of our repentance, such as feeling sorrow for our sins or abandoning them, may not be visible to others. In fact, most people are probably unaware of our sins or our need to repent. Confessing our transgressions, then, may be a difficult condition of our repentance. It will test the depth of our humility. But it is a required condition—every sin must be confessed. The Lord declared, "By this ye may know if a man repenteth of his sins—behold, he will confess them and forsake them" (D&C 58:43).

We feel immediate relief after we confess our transgressions. Confession frees us from being trapped in sin by exposing our sins to light and loosening the binding cords of the adversary. The weight of hiding our iniquities and of living a lie is lifted, and a critical barrier keeping us from repenting and receiving forgiveness is broken. Hope replaces despair. We can now look forward to being clean again and free of sin's oppressive burden; we can see the day when we will be filled with peace and when our confidence will once again "wax strong in the presence of God" (D&C 121:45).

The Psalmist wrote, "I will declare mine iniquity" (Psalm 38:18). But to whom do we confess our sins? Figuratively speaking, we have already confessed our transgressions to ourselves by recognizing our sins. We must now confess our transgressions to the Lord, to those we sinned against, and perhaps even to our bishop.

CONFESSING TO GOD

We are commanded to confess all our sins to our Father in Heaven. Ezra, an Old Testament priest and scribe, instructed the people assembled at Jerusalem to "make confession unto the Lord God" (Ezra 10:11). The Lord Himself said, "I, the Lord, forgive sins unto those who confess their sins before me and ask forgiveness" (D&C 64:7).

After members have confessed their sins to me, I ask them, "Have you confessed your sins to the Lord?" A surprising number have not or have confessed only in general terms. I then counsel them: "You need to confess your sins to the Lord. Be totally honest when you confess. Don't sugarcoat your actions or your feelings. Tell your Father in Heaven everything; withhold nothing."

The Lord "is a rewarder of them that diligently seek him" (Hebrews 11:6). He will strengthen our resolve and ability to overcome our sins when we diligently confess our sins to Him—when our confessions are thorough, specific, and free of all the elements of pride.

CONFESSING TO OTHERS

We are to confess our sins to those we have sinned against. James taught, "Confess your faults one to another" (James 5:16). Alma the Younger and the sons of Mosiah, whose sins severely affected many people, "traveled throughout all the land . . . confessing all their sins" (Mosiah 27:35). There is no need, however, to confess our minor sins to others when our transgressions are only between us and the Lord. President Brigham Young counseled,

> Tell to the public that which belongs to the public. If you have sinned against the people, confess to them. If you have sinned against a family or a neighborhood, go to them and confess. If you have sinned against your ward, confess to your ward. If you have sinned against one individual, take that person by yourselves and make your confession to him. And if you have sinned against your God, or against yourselves, confess to God, and keep the matter to yourselves, for I do not want to know anything about it.[1]

MAKING CONFESSION

CONFESSING TO OUR BISHOP

We must confess our serious sins to our bishop. A serious sin is a transgression that may affect our privileges of Church membership. Elder Marion G. Romney stated,

> Where one's transgressions are of such a nature as would, unrepented of, put in jeopardy his right to membership or fellowship in the Church of Jesus Christ, full and effective confession would, in my judgment, require confession by the repentant sinner to his bishop or other proper presiding Church officer.[2]

You should consider, as a useful guide, talking with your bishop about any sin you have committed that keeps you from properly answering a temple recommend question. You may also want to talk with your bishop if you are tempted to commit a serious sin. He can give you inspired counsel that will help strengthen you in resisting the sin. It is much better to speak with your bishop before you transgress than after. "Call me," I have pled with members, "if you're in a dangerous situation or tempted to do wrong." Your bishop's love and support may be the help you need to conquer Satan and his temptations.

One of a bishop's responsibilities is to hear confessions and, when appropriate, to administer Church discipline. Church discipline helps transgressors recognize the magnitude of their sins and fulfill the conditions of their repentance. One form of Church discipline, for example, is to prohibit a transgressor from partaking of the sacrament. Jesus taught His disciples: "Ye shall not suffer any one knowingly to partake of my flesh and blood unworthily" (3 Nephi 18:28). The bishop has the same charge. He also has duties similar to those given by the Lord to the prophet Alma:

> Whosoever transgresseth against me, him shall ye judge according to the sins which he has committed; and if he confess his sins before thee and me, and repenteth in the sincerity of his heart, him shall ye forgive, and I will forgive him also.
>
> Now I say unto you, Go; and whosoever will not repent of his sins the same shall not be numbered among my people; and this shall be observed from this time forward.

And it came to pass that Alma went and judged those that had been taken in iniquity, according to the word of the Lord.

And whosoever repented of their sins and did confess them, them he did number among the people of the church;

And those that would not confess their sins and repent of their iniquity, the same were not numbered among the people of the church, and their names were blotted out. (Mosiah 26:29, 32, 34–36)

If you have committed a serious sin, do not delay in confessing your sin to your bishop. You can overcome a small sin on your own—just as you can handle a small cut with a simple bandage. But with a large gash you need to be under the care of a doctor, and with a serious sin you need the help of your bishop. Your bishop will assist you with love and compassion. He will keep your confession and transgression confidential.[3] Your bishop is your friend; he will not condemn or criticize you. He wants you to be happy and worthy to return to our Father in Heaven. He will seek inspiration from the Lord to know how best to help you repent.

CONFESSING WITH A HUMBLE HEART

"What a difference," wrote Elder Spencer W. Kimball, "between admission and confession!"[4] God promised mercy and forgiveness to "those who confess their sins with humble hearts" (D&C 61:2). A humble and voluntary confession demonstrates our recognition of wrongdoing, our sorrow for the sin and the hurt we caused to others, and our desire to take responsibility for our actions and to make restitution. And, unlike an admission of guilt after we have been confronted with factual evidence of our transgression, a sincere confession is motivated by a true desire to be clean and free from sin; it is motivated by "godly sorrow" (2 Corinthians 7:10). President J. Reuben Clark Jr., formerly of the First Presidency, said: "There is a great difference between confession and admission, after transgression is proved. I doubt much the efficacy of an admission as a confession."[5]

KEPT BACK PART

Without a humble heart, we will be tempted to minimize or to give an incomplete accounting of our sins. Do not fall into this defensive trap of pride. When we confess, we need to confess completely. We should never dilute or misrepresent our sins for any reason—even if we feel embarrassed, fear we will disappoint others, or want to avoid the full penalty of our sins. Anything other than a true and thorough confession is, of course, another sin—it is a lie. An incomplete confession indicates we are not ready to fully repent and have yet to experience "a broken heart and a contrite spirit" (2 Nephi 2:7).

The story of Ananias and his wife, Sapphira, and their deceit in professing to live the law of consecration provides a poignant example of the Lord's requirement for us to be completely open and honest with His servants:

> But a certain man named Ananias, with Sapphira his wife, sold a possession, and kept back part of the price, his wife also being privy to it, and brought a certain part, and laid it at the apostles' feet.
>
> But Peter said, Ananias, why hath Satan filled thine heart to lie to the Holy Ghost, and to keep back part of the price of the land? Whiles it remained, was it not thine own? and after it was sold, was it not in thine own power? why hast thou conceived this thing in thine heart? thou hast not lied unto men, but unto God.
>
> And Ananias hearing these words fell down, and gave up the ghost: and great fear came on all them that heard these things. And the young men arose, wound him up, and carried him out, and buried him.
>
> And it was about the space of three hours after, when his wife, not knowing what was done, came in. And Peter answered unto her, Tell me whether ye sold the land for so much? And she said, Yea, for so much. Then Peter said unto her, How is it that ye have agreed together to tempt the Spirit of the Lord? behold, the feet of them which have buried thy husband are at the door, and shall carry thee out.
>
> Then fell she down straightway at his feet, and yielded up the ghost: and the young men came in, and found her dead, and, carrying her forth, buried her by her husband.
>
> And great fear came upon all the church, and upon as many as heard these things. (Acts 5:1–11)

It has been my experience that if you have previously confessed to only a portion of a prior serious sin, you will, after your testimony has grown and significant events have unfolded in your life, want to complete your confession and gain full forgiveness from the Lord. Maybe you will fall in love and become engaged to be married. You will, prior to your sealing, go to your bishop and say, "Bishop, I'm getting married to my best friend. I want to be totally clean before the Lord and for my eternal companion. I want more than a temple marriage; I want an eternal marriage. I was too shy to disclose everything to my previous bishop. Can we talk?" Perhaps you will be blessed with beautiful children. You will go to your bishop and say, "Bishop, the Lord has blessed me with a beautiful family. I can't imagine spending eternity without them! So I've come to confess everything about a previous sin. I want to be worthy so I can be with them forever." Or maybe an aged parent or friend, whom you love and adore, will pass away. Their death will cause you to review your life. You will then go to your bishop and say, "I have some things I never fully confessed. I'd like to do so now."

Elder Spencer W. Kimball wrote, "Incomplete repentance never brought complete forgiveness."[6] The opposite, of course, is also true: complete repentance—including a full confession—brings us complete forgiveness.

EVERY TONGUE SHALL CONFESS

Confessing our sins is a commandment of the Lord. We can confess our sins now, delay until later in life, or wait until Final Judgment. But we will all eventually confess. Paul taught the Romans,

> We shall all stand before the judgment seat of Christ.
> For it is written, As I live, saith the Lord, every knee shall bow to me, and every tongue shall confess to God.
> So then every one of us shall give account of himself to God. (Romans 14:10–12)

The longer we delay our confessions, the longer we will be "heavy laden" (Matthew 11:28) with the burden of our unrepented sins. Elder Vaughn J. Featherstone, while serving as a stake president, visited with a couple who completed, rather than started, their repentance with confession. As a consequence, they had carried the burden of their sin for many, many years:

> Some years ago, a man knocked on my office door late at night and said, "President, may I speak to you? Are we all alone?" I assured him no one else was in the office. We sat across the corner of the desk, and he said, "Four times I have driven over to the stake office and have seen your light on, and four times I have driven back home without coming in. But," he continued, "last night I was reading in *The Miracle of Forgiveness* again, and I realized that every major transgression must be confessed. I have come to confess a transgression." . . .
>
> He said, "Forty-two years ago, before my wife and I were married, we committed fornication once, the week prior to our going to the temple. We did not lie to the bishop, who was my wife's father; he simply talked with us and signed our recommends. We then went to the stake president, and he did not interview us. He signed our recommends, and we went to the temple unworthily. While we were on our honeymoon," he continued, "we decided to make it up to the Lord. We decided we would pay more than our share of tithing and more than our share of building fund; we would accept every assignment to the welfare farm and do all else we were asked to do. We decided we were not worthy to go to the temple, and we did not go for a year. It has been forty-two years since the transgression, and we have lived as near Christlike lives as we know how. I believe we have been forgiven, but I know that confession is necessary."
>
> Then he quoted from 2 Nephi 9:41, which states, "Behold, the way for man is narrow, but it lieth in a straight course before him, and the keeper of the gate is the Holy One of Israel; and he employeth no servant there; and there is none other way save it be by the gate; for he cannot be deceived, for the Lord God is his name."
>
> Then he said, "I would rather confess to you now. I am not a young man, and I do not have a lot of years left. I want to be able to meet my Savior with nothing left undone."
>
> I listened to his confession. I wept with him, and when he finished the confession, I told him on behalf of the Church that he was forgiven. He need not discuss it, think about it, or be concerned about it anymore. I told him never to mention it to me again, for I would not remember it and had no desire to. To this day, I cannot remember who it was, although I do remember the case.

We got up and walked to the door together. I said, "Where is your wife?"

He said, "She is in the car."

I asked, "Is she coming in?"

He replied, "No, she can't even think about it except it almost destroys her."

I said, "You tell your wife that I would like to visit with her now. Tell her I want to take this off her heart and close it. Tell her I know what it was that was done, and I will close it, and it need not be opened again. Tell her I will make it as easy as possible for her."

He said, "I'll tell her, but I don't think she will come in."

I answered, "You tell her that if I have to sit here all night, I will not go home until she comes in. I can't bear the thought of her carrying this on her heart one more day in this life; forty-two years is long enough."

He said, "Well, I'll tell her, but I don't think she'll come in."

He left and was gone fifteen minutes, thirty minutes, and forty-five minutes. I was tempted to check the parking lot to see if they had gone home. I resisted; then I heard a timid knock at the door. I went to the door, and there was this sweet woman standing there. Her eyes were wet from crying. She had probably told her husband she couldn't come in. He had insisted, telling her I would stay there all night. Finally, forty-five minutes later, she was at the door. I took her by both hands and led her across the room. I sat across the corner of the desk, and then I said, "Your husband confessed to a transgression that happened over forty-two years ago of which you were a part. I want to make it easy for you. I know what the transgression is. Every major transgression must be confessed. You tell me, and I will take it off your heart."

It was like pulling wild horses to get a confession. Finally, about fifteen minutes later, she confessed. I wept; she wept. I told her it was closed and that I wouldn't remember it and for her to forget it and close it. Then I stood up and put my arm through hers and we walked down the long hallway to the parking lot. When we got just about to the door, I said, "How do you feel?"

She stopped, looked up at me and, with tears in her eyes, and said, "President, I feel clean for the first time in forty-two years."[7]

There is no divine forgiveness without confession. If you are laboring under the burden of sin, you can be immediately relieved of some of the burden by confessing your sins today—to the Lord, to those you sinned against, and, if necessary, to your bishop.

NOTES

1. Brigham Young, in *Journal of Discourses* (London: Latter-day Saints' Book Depot, 1861), 8:362; spelling and capitalization modernized.
2. Marion G. Romney, in Conference Report, October 1955, 125.
3. In some areas a bishop may be required to report child abuse and neglect to civil authorities.
4. Spencer W. Kimball, *The Miracle of Forgiveness* (Salt Lake City: Bookcraft, 1969), 310.
5. J. Reuben Clark Jr., in Conference Report, April 1950, 166.
6. Kimball, *The Miracle of Forgiveness*, 212.
7. Vaughn J. Featherstone, "'Forgive Them, I Pray Thee,'" *Ensign*, November 1980, 30.

PROVIDING RESTITUTION: HE
Shall RECOMPENSE *His* TRESPASS

*H*E SHALL RECOMPENSE his trespass" (Numbers 5:7), declared the Lord. Making restitution for our sins is a vital and necessary condition of our repentance. Without restitution, confessing our transgressions and expressing remorse are hollow and meaningless gestures. Elder Orson Pratt said, "You may confess your sins; but if you never make restitution to the persons you have wronged, your confession will be of no service."[1]

Zacchaeus, a chief tax collector[2] at Jericho, was too short to see over the crowd of people thronging to catch a glimpse of Jesus, so he ran ahead and climbed a sycamore tree to get a better view:

> And when Jesus came to the place, he looked up, and saw him, and said unto him, Zacchaeus, make haste, and come down; for to day I must abide at thy house. And he made haste, and came down, and received him joyfully.
>
> And when they saw it, they all murmured, saying, That he was gone to be guest with a man that is a sinner.
>
> And Zacchaeus stood, and said unto the Lord; Behold, Lord, the half of my goods I give to the poor; and if I have taken any thing from any man by false accusation, I restore him fourfold. And Jesus said unto him, This day is salvation come to this house. (Luke 19:5–9)

Zacchaeus vowed to make restitution for his sins—and to do so generously. He committed not only to giving half his wealth to the poor but also to restoring fourfold to anyone he had defrauded or cheated. The law of Moses only required him to "restore . . . the principal, and . . . add the fifth part more thereto" (Leviticus 6:5) for "the thing which he hath deceitfully gotten" (Leviticus 6:4), but the repentant Zacchaeus voluntarily followed a stricter portion of the law and offered a fourfold restitution.[3]

REPAIR ALL THE INJURIES

When we "zealously strive to repair all the injuries" (Mosiah 27:35; tense changed) we have done, we demonstrate to the Lord and to those we have hurt that we truly regret our sinful actions. Ideally, we will become fully aware of the harm we caused so that we can, if possible, make complete amends (or, like Zacchaeus, make an even greater restitution). For example, if we have stolen from someone, we must, of course, return or pay for the stolen items. But we should also make up for any other loss that the person suffered because of our theft. To illustrate this point, consider the following true story about a young man we'll call Jake.

Jake and his friend were arrested for breaking into a neighbor's home and stealing several valuable possessions—including some that had sentimental value to the family. In addition to losing their personal property, the family's young son lost his sense of security. He feared the thieves would return, and he could no longer sleep soundly at night.

To make amends for his crime, Jake contributed money toward the value of the stolen belongings. He realized, however, he could not make a full restitution because of the personal value attached to some of the items. Jake also understood restitution required more than his financial compensation, as he described in his letter of apology:

> I know that saying sorry will not bring back any of the items that were taken from your home, nor will it help your five-year-old son get to sleep at night without having to make sure that the doors are locked. . . .
>
> I can't go back in time and undo what was done, because believe me I would. I'm sorry that I did not think about the consequences of my actions. I'm sorry that I did not think about the

extent of the hurt that would come to you and your family because of my actions. I cannot tell you in words how much it saddens me to know that a five-year-old boy cannot sleep at night because of what I did, but I hope that the night-light that I gave him makes a difference, even if it's only a little one. I only wish that I would've known the hurt that I caused before I did what I did. I never, ever would have done it.

In closing I only ask that you somehow can find it in your heart to forgive me for my actions and for the pain that I caused you and your family.[4]

When we are truly repentant, like Jake in the story above, we want to repair not only the physical but also the emotional damage caused by our transgressions. We do everything we can to help those we have sinned against regain their trust in us. We also strive to restore their trust in people or organizations we represent, such as our family, friends, and the Church. We seek to assist them in rebuilding their faith in God and in recovering their sense of justice if their beliefs were weakened by our iniquities. And if their good names have been tarnished by our careless or malicious words, we do all in our power to repair their reputations.

Our complete restitution—including our compliance with any long-term obligations—can help others forgive us of our transgressions and find peace of mind; it can give them confidence that we have forsaken our unrighteous acts and will never again commit the same offenses against them or anyone else.

RESTITUTION AND SINS OF OMISSION

Most of the conditions of repentance for sins of omission are the same as those for sins of commission. We should feel sorrow for our lack of doing good, confess our neglect of duty, and ask forgiveness. But how do we make restitution?

Sins of omission are usually lost opportunities—opportunities which are difficult, if not impossible, to recover. We may be able to make up tithing not paid, but how do we make up for Sabbaths not kept holy, prayers not said, or children not fully taught the gospel? How do we make restitution for neglecting our home and visiting teaching or failing to share the gospel?

Unfortunately, sometimes we cannot make complete amends. Elder Spencer W. Kimball stated,

> It is obvious that the murderer cannot give back a life he has taken; the libertine [immoral individual] cannot restore the virtue he has violated; the gossip may be unable to nullify and overcome the evils done by a loose tongue; but, so far as is possible, one must restore and make good the damage done.[5]

Even when full restitution is impossible, we can still find forgiveness. President Joseph F. Smith taught, "When we cannot make restitution for the wrong we have done, then we must apply for the grace and mercy of God to cleanse us from that iniquity."[6] And we must continue to keep the commandments, for our "subsequent example of righteousness," explained Elder Neal A. Maxwell, "provides a compensatory form of restitution."[7]

Our restitution for our sins of omission, then, is tightly bound with forsaking our sins—meaning we must abandon our slothfulness and "bring forth works of righteousness" (Alma 5:35). We must now be completely faithful in our obedience to the commandments; we must from this time forward "be steadfast and immovable, always abounding in good works" (Mosiah 5:15). The Lord declared, "Let every man be diligent in all things. And the idler shall not have place in the church, except he repent and mend his ways" (D&C 75:29).

In the parable of the two sons, told by Jesus to the chief priests and elders of the people, the first son initially refused his father's call to go and work in the vineyard. But he forsook his sin of omission and went to work. His brother, however, neither worked nor repented:

> But what think ye? A certain man had two sons; and he came to the first, and said, Son, go work to day in my vineyard.
>
> He answered and said, I will not: but afterward he repented, and went.
>
> And he came to the second, and said likewise. And he answered and said, I go, sir: and went not.
>
> Whether of them twain did the will of his father? They say unto him, The first. Jesus saith unto them, Verily I say unto you, That the publicans and the harlots [being likened to the first son] go into the kingdom of God before you. (Matthew 21:28–31)

"The first son," wrote Elder James E. Talmage, "relented and set to work, repentantly hoping to make amends for the time he had lost and for the unfilial [disrespectful] spirit he had shown."[8] His restitution consisted of abandoning his sin and laboring diligently in his father's vineyard.

RESTORE THE PLEDGE

Our restitution, when possible, must be equal to or greater than the effects of our sins. But if we have repeatedly committed the same sin against the same person, then our restitution must be much more. Like the substantial restitution specified in the law of Moses, the Lord revealed through Joseph Smith that our multiple transgressions "shall not be blotted out until [we] repent and reward . . . four-fold in all things" (D&C 98:44) to those we have trespassed against. Our fourfold reparation serves to both punish us for our repeated evil and, like Zacchaeus, to make abundant restitution to the injured.

Only when we make a willing and appropriate restitution can we be forgiven of our sins. The Lord told the prophet Ezekiel: "If the wicked restore the pledge, give again that he had robbed, walk in the statutes of life, without committing iniquity; he shall surely live. . . . None of his sins that he hath committed shall be mentioned unto him" (Ezekiel 33:15–16).

TWO NOTES OF CAUTION

If you have committed serious transgressions against others, you may desire to ask their forgiveness and to make restitution when you should not or perhaps may not legally contact them. Your desire to provide restitution should never cause them additional grief or pain. Those injured by your sins may not be ready to receive you, and your efforts to redress your wrongs may only reopen wounds that have not fully healed.

If you have broken laws of the land, making restitution may require you to report your illegal activities to a civil authority. Before doing so, however, you should receive competent legal advice.

NOTES

1. Orson Pratt, in *Journal of Discourses* (London: Latter-day Saints' Book Depot, 1860), 7:263.
2. Publicans, or tax collectors, were despised by their fellow Jews and considered traitors and sinners for associating with their pagan Roman occupiers. They were hired by wealthy Romans to collect a fixed amount of taxes for Rome from their local districts. Any funds they collected above the amount they had contracted with their employer they kept as profit—leading to extortion, overcharging, and further angering the people.
3. The theft of a sheep required a fourfold restitution if it was killed or sold; an ox was reimbursed fivefold (see Exodus 22:1–4). In addition to being a source of food, livestock was used in generating family income. The potential harm to a family's livelihood was considered a greater loss than wealth taken through extortion or fraud. Zacchaeus, perhaps, treated his theft "by false accusation" equal to the theft of livestock and increased his restitution substantially.
4. "A Letter from a Young Person," *Calgary Community Conferencing Newsletter*, October 2001, 2; grammar altered.
5. Spencer W. Kimball, in Conference Report, October 1949, 128.
6. Joseph F. Smith, *Gospel Doctrine* (Salt Lake City: Deseret Book, 1986), 98.
7. Neal A. Maxwell, "Repentance," *Ensign*, November 1991, 31.
8. James E. Talmage, *Jesus the Christ* (Salt Lake City: The Church of Jesus Christ of Latter-day Saints, 1981), 532.

DEMONSTRATING OBEDIENCE:
FROM *This* TIME FORTH

*I*CAN JUST APPLY the Atonement again," implied the lifelong member while he casually explained how he would recover from the latest repetition of his sin. He seemed to think he could sin, confess, and ask forgiveness as often as necessary—as if repentance was nothing more than a simple confession and a temporary abandonment of wrongdoing.

The Nicolaitans, a religious group mentioned in the book of Revelation, had a similar, but certainly more corrupt, understanding of the Atonement. They believed Christ's infinite grace allowed them to freely and repeatedly commit sexual and other sins and still be saved in the kingdom of God. The Apostle Paul previously denounced this false doctrine, writing, "Shall we continue in sin, that grace may abound? God forbid" (Romans 6:1–2). The Lord was more direct. He revealed to His leaders in Asia that the deeds and doctrines of the Nicolaitans are "thing[s] I hate" (Revelation 2:15; see also verse 6).

God will forgive our sins when we abandon them and keep His commandments "from this time forth" (D&C 88:76). But our change must be permanent—we cannot continue to sin. Isaiah taught, "Let the wicked forsake his way, . . . and let him return unto the Lord, and he will have mercy upon him; and . . . he will abundantly pardon" (Isaiah 55:7).

The people of Ammon gave us a striking example of permanently casting off "the works of darkness" (Romans 13:12). After they were converted and received forgiveness for their "many sins and murders" (Alma 24:10), they buried their weapons as "a testimony to God, and also to men" that they would no longer be a warring people. "This they did," wrote Mormon, "vouching and covenanting with God, that rather than shed the blood of their brethren they would give up their own lives" (Alma 24:18). Mormon later affirmed that "they had entered into a covenant and *they would not break it*" (Alma 43:11; emphasis added).

Elder Glen L. Rudd, formerly of the Seventy, shared the following story of immediately and permanently abandoning sin:

> There was a man by the name of Syd who lived in a little Maori village on the east coast of New Zealand. At that time there was a large branch of the Church there with about four hundred members. One Saturday afternoon, after a long, eight-hour drive, President Matthew Cowley arrived at this village and went directly to see his old friend, Syd. . . .
>
> Syd had been ordained a seventy [when there were seventies quorums in the stakes of the Church] while he had lived in the United States, and when he arrived back in New Zealand, he had found that he was the only seventy in the whole area, and he didn't have a quorum to belong to. He had become somewhat inactive, and he hadn't been keeping the Word of Wisdom, but deep within his heart he still knew the gospel to be true.
>
> As a mission president and a friend, President Cowley called on Syd, and found him sitting in a rocking chair on his front porch, smoking a big cigar. Syd didn't stop chewing on his cigar as President Cowley sat down beside him to visit.
>
> After they had talked and laughed for a while, President Cowley became serious and said, "Syd, I want you to come to church tomorrow."
>
> They both looked toward the old chapel, and Syd said, "I think it'll fall in if I do. I haven't been there for a long time. I don't think I'd better risk it."
>
> President Cowley said, "Syd, I want you to be there. I'm going to do something important tomorrow."
>
> Syd inquired, "What are you going to do?"

President Cowley answered, "I'm going to release the branch president and put in a new one."

Syd said, "I haven't been there for a long time. Why don't you just tell me who the new branch president will be, and then I won't have to get myself cleaned up for church in the morning."

President Cowley said, "Well, I'll tell you who it is. It's going to be you."

Syd pulled that old cigar out of his mouth, looked at it, and said, "President, you mean me and my cigar?"

President Cowley said, "No, Syd—just you. We don't need your cigar."

Then Syd threw the cigar out on the ground in front of the porch. He thought for a minute, turned to President Cowley, and very humbly said, "President, I won't break the Word of Wisdom any more. I'm a full-tithe payer. I'll be the branch president, and I'll be worthy. Tomorrow morning I'll be there, and I promise you that I'll be the best branch president in the whole country. You won't have to worry about me and whether or not I'm living the gospel."

For the next several years, Syd served as one of the strongest and finest leaders in the mission. . . . Syd's whole family is strong and active in the Church today and is one of the great families in New Zealand.[1]

ENTANGLED AGAIN

Will God forgive us again if we repeat a sin we repented of earlier? Yes, but perhaps not every time and certainly not without consequences.

The Lord declared, "As often as my people repent will I forgive them their trespasses against me" (Mosiah 26:30). And Moroni wrote, "As oft as they repented and sought forgiveness, with real intent, they were forgiven" (Moroni 6:8). These scriptures undoubtedly refer to the many different sins we commit, but they may also refer to sins previously forsaken. We cannot, however, be indifferent about repeated transgressions. Joseph Smith taught:

> Repentance is a thing that cannot be trifled with every day. Daily transgression and daily repentance is not . . . pleasing in the sight of God.[2]

Not only is the Lord not pleased when we treat sin and repentance as though they were separated by a revolving door, but we are warned to "sin no more" and "unto that soul who sinneth shall the former sins return" (D&C 82:7). When we repeat a supposedly abandoned sin, our forgiveness for our former sin is withdrawn, and we must repent anew. Our change of heart was incomplete, and we yielded again to Satan and broke our covenant of obedience. Our past sin is now added to our new one, and the Lord may require more of us to receive forgiveness under our new conditions of repentance than He did when we first repented.

Below are three examples illustrating the consequences of repeated sin. The severity of the consequences varies according to the sin and the individual's true desire to repent.

Repeating Minor Sins. In his 1832 account of the First Vision, Joseph Smith gave an explanation for his purpose in going to the grove to pray that is not recorded in the Pearl of Great Price. He wrote, "I became convicted of my sins. . . . Therefore, I cried unto the Lord for mercy." When the Lord appeared to Joseph, he was told (along with other important instructions, of course), "Joseph, my son, thy sins are forgiven thee."[3] Some time afterwards, Joseph again fell into minor youthful temptations that were "offensive in the sight of God" (Joseph Smith—History 1:28). The scriptures record:

> After it was truly manifested unto [Joseph] that he had received a remission of his sins [in the First Vision], he was entangled again in the vanities of the world; but after repenting, and humbling himself sincerely, through faith, God ministered unto him by an holy angel. (D&C 20:5–6)

Oliver Cowdery wrote that Moroni—the holy angel—came "to deliver a special message" and to witness to Joseph "that his sins were [again] forgiven, and that his prayers were heard."[4]

Violating the Law of Chastity. Alma cautioned his son Corianton, "Do not risk one more offense against your God upon those points of doctrine [sexual purity], which ye have hitherto risked to commit sin" (Alma 41:9). The Lord also warned against "one more offense" when He "[spoke] unto the church" (D&C 42:18) about the sin of adultery:

> He that has committed adultery and repents with all his heart, and forsaketh it, and doeth it no more, thou shalt forgive; but if he

doeth it again, he shall not be forgiven, but shall be cast out. (D&C 42:25–26)

Refusing to Forsake Sinful Desires and Actions. Lot and his family were warned to "look not behind [them]" (Genesis 19:17) by the holy men escorting them out of Sodom. Lot's wife, however, "looked back," and "she became a pillar of salt" (Genesis 19:26). The Lord gave the same commandment in modern revelation: "Go ye out . . . from the midst of wickedness, . . . and he that goeth, let him not look back lest sudden destruction shall come upon him" (D&C 133:14–15).

SINS OF ADDICTION

Sins of addiction, such as substance dependencies, pornography, and gambling, may be particularly difficult to overcome. Do not let Satan discourage you as you fight to be free from your sin. It may take time and you may relapse, but you can overcome your addiction. Consult with your bishop—he can give you inspired counsel and words of love and encouragement. Seek out a competent counselor and an addiction recovery program if you need professional help. And, of course, do those things that will help you feel the Spirit and give you spiritual strength—say your prayers, fast, study the scriptures, and attend church.

Many times sins of addiction or other reoccurring sins are rooted in our weaknesses. While weaknesses are not sins (in fact, they are given to us from the Lord to keep us humble—see Ether 12:27), they can lead us to commit sin if we are not careful. If we have a personal weakness that contributes to our succumbing to temptation, such as an emotional characteristic or behavioral tendency, we may need to better understand or resolve our weakness before we can successfully repent.

For example, I met with a member who said, "Bishop, I pray every day and attend church weekly, yet I cannot overcome my quick temper." I asked him, "Besides praying and going to church, what else are you doing?" He answered, "That's what I'm doing, and it's not working."

"You're not applying a basic principle," I responded. "The Lord will not do for you what you can do for yourself. First, you must learn as much as you can about why you are easily angered, meaning you need to understand any characteristics or weaknesses you have that contribute to your quick temper. Then you must learn what techniques or tools you can use to overcome those weaknesses. And, finally, you must put into practice what you've learned.

"Let me give you an example," I continued. "I like to play racquetball, and I'd like to be a better player. If I pray daily and attend church weekly, will I become a better player?"

He answered, "Of course not!"

"Exactly," I said. "The Lord may inspire me to take lessons, or to practice, or to do both, but He won't increase my ability simply because I ask Him. I have to do my part."

The Lord stated, "Search diligently, pray always, and be believing, and all things shall work together for your good" (D&C 90:24). Searching diligently means we do all we can before expecting God's help. In a revelation given through Joseph Smith, the Lord counseled Oliver Cowdery:

> You have supposed that I would give it unto you, when you took no thought save it was to ask me. But, behold, I say unto you, that you must study it out in your mind; then you must ask me. (D&C 9:7–8)

If your bishop recommends that you consider professional counseling to help you overcome a weakness or sin, take his advice seriously. There is no shame in trying to become better by seeking help from someone who has the appropriate expertise. We do this all the time—we go to school, enroll in job training courses, take music (or racquetball) lessons, and attend church. Learning how to increase our abilities and enrich our lives through professional counseling is no different.

TIME AND AGENCY

Unfortunately, many times after a brief renewed vigor to keep the commandments we are, as Mormon observed of the Nephites, quick to "forget the Lord" and "quick to do iniquity, and to be led away by the evil one" (Alma 46:8). Or, in Mormon's more descriptive words, we have "turned from [our] righteousness, like the dog to his vomit, or like the sow to her wallowing in the mire" (3 Nephi 7:8).

The passage of time without another offense against the broken commandment is one of the best witnesses that we are true to our "covenant with [God] to keep his commandments" (Alma 7:15). But it is not just the passing of time that confirms we have repented. We cannot simply wait for some prescribed sin-free season to elapse before we receive forgiveness. We must be busy strengthening our determination to always be obedient and fortifying our change of heart.

We must also be free to exercise our agency to prove we have forsaken our sins by demonstrating we can both avoid and resist temptation. Elder Spencer W. Kimball wrote:

> Repentance is inseparable from time. No one can repent on the cross, nor in prison, nor in custody. One must have the opportunity of committing wrong in order to be really repentant.[5]

I once met a man who had been excommunicated from the Church for promiscuity. After many years, he desired to reunite with the Church because, he said, he had become too old to chase women. Perhaps he did not sincerely forsake his sin but simply lost the energy to sin. True repentance is abandoning our sins, in both thought and deed, while we have the opportunity to sin. If the opportunity is past, we must be sure our change of heart is genuine and complete. There is a relevant prison saying that questions an inmate's commitment to be law abiding after his freedom is restored: "Born again till out again."

Korihor, the anti-Christ, acknowledged his sins while he was deprived of his agency, but he did not repent. He was cursed by the Lord with the inability to speak (and apparently hear) for leading the people into wickedness and for seeking a sign of God's existence. After being stricken he wrote Alma, confessing: "I always knew that there was a God. But behold, the devil hath deceived me; . . . And I have taught his words" (Alma 30:52–53). He then asked Alma to pray that his curse would be removed. But Alma replied, "If this curse should be taken from thee thou wouldst again lead away the hearts of this people" (Alma 30:55). Korihor had not forsaken his sins but was simply kept from sinning. He would have sinned again if his voice and hearing had been restored.

The Lord did not come to redeem us *in* our sins but *from* our sins (see Helaman 5:10); we are "not excusable in [our] transgressions" (D&C 24:2). After the accusers of the adulteress departed under the guilt of their own sins, Jesus told her, "Neither do I condemn thee: go, and sin no more" (John 8:11). He did not condemn her, but to receive forgiveness she needed to fulfill all the conditions of her repentance—which included forsaking her sin.

The Lord promises us forgiveness and eternal life when we forsake our sins and keep His "commandments from henceforth" (D&C 96:6). He declared,

> Verily, thus saith the Lord: It shall come to pass that every soul who forsaketh his sins and cometh unto me, and calleth on my name, and obeyeth my voice, and keepeth my commandments, shall see my face and know that I am. (D&C 93:1)

NOTES

1. Glen L. Rudd, "Keeping the Gospel Simple," *Ensign*, January 1989, 72–73; combined with Glen L. Rudd, "Keeping the Gospel Simple," *Tambuli*, March 1990, 24.

2. Joseph Smith, *History of the Church of Jesus Christ of Latter-day Saints* (Salt Lake City: The Church of Jesus Christ of Latter-day Saints, 1948), 3:379.

3. Joseph Smith, in *Histories, Volume 1:1832–1844*, vol. 1 of the Histories series of *The Joseph Smith Papers* (Salt Lake City: Church Historians Press, 2012), 11–13; tense changed, grammar and capitalization modernized.

4. Oliver Cowdery, *Latter Day Saints' Messenger and Advocate*, February 1835, 79.

5. Spencer W. Kimball, *The Miracle of Forgiveness* (Salt Lake City: Bookcraft, 1969), 167–68.

RENEWING COVENANTS:
FULFILLING *the* COMMANDMENTS

*W*HILE CONVERSING WITH Moses face-to-face, the Lord told His prophet, "This is my work and my glory—to bring to pass the immortality and eternal life of man" (Moses 1:39). He has also revealed to us our mission: "This is your work, to keep my commandments, yea, with all your might, mind and strength" (D&C 11:20).

Before we were baptized we repented of all our sins, and we demonstrated our willingness to make sacred covenants by obeying all God's commandments. When we commit sins after our baptism, we must renew our covenant to observe all the commandments in order to receive divine forgiveness. We cannot choose to ignore or disobey some of God's laws while we are repenting of others. "He that repents and does the commandments," said the Lord, "shall be forgiven" (D&C 1:32).

A sister, who was repenting of a major sexual transgression, made an important observation about obedience during one of our interviews. She said, "When we start living the law of chastity, we also need to look at the types of music we listen to, the kinds of television shows and movies we watch, and how we dress." The Spirit had taught her the law of chastity was more than abstaining from sexual intimacy before marriage. She learned that she needed to accept and live the entire commandment. She also began to understand her complete change of heart would lead her to faithfully obey every commandment.

King Lamoni's father, who was king over all the Lamanites, provides us another example of being willing to be obedient to all the commandments. He drew his sword and tried to kill Ammon for his role in King Lamoni's conversion, but Ammon defended himself and wounded the old king. King Lamoni's father then bargained with Ammon for his life, saying, "If thou wilt spare me I will grant unto thee whatsoever thou wilt ask, *even to half of the kingdom*" (Alma 20:23; emphasis added). Some time later, and after Ammon's brother, Aaron, taught him of the Creation, the Fall, and the plan of redemption, the king was willing to give up significantly more—even all that he had. He asked Aaron,

> What shall I do that I may have this eternal life of which thou hast spoken? Yea, what shall I do that I may be born of God, having this wicked spirit rooted out of my breast, and receive his Spirit, that I may be filled with joy, that I may not be cast off at the last day? Behold, . . . *I will give up all that I possess, yea, I will forsake my kingdom*, that I may receive this great joy. (Alma 22:15; emphasis added)

His desires to receive great joy and to inherit eternal life were so strong that he was ready to sacrifice all he possessed to obtain them. Although his willingness was remarkable, Aaron taught the king that instead of forsaking his kingdom, he needed to forsake all his sins:

> If thou wilt repent of all thy sins, and will bow down before God, and call on his name in faith, believing that ye shall receive, then shalt thou receive the hope which thou desirest. (Alma 22:16)

King Lamoni's father then prayed and promised the Lord, "I will give away *all* my sins to know thee" (Alma 22:18; emphasis added). He understood true repentance involved abandoning all his sins and keeping all the commandments. In fact, after his conversion, he sent out a decree among his people directing them to not interfere with the missionaries preaching the gospel—hoping his people would be converted and no longer "commit *any* manner of wickedness" (Alma 23:3; emphasis added).

BEARING TESTIMONY TO ALL THE WORLD

After we have received forgiveness of our sins and "have felt to sing the song of redeeming love" (Alma 5:26), we will naturally desire "to stand as witnesses of God at all times and in all things" (Mosiah 18:9). We will want to testify to others of the infinite Atonement of Jesus Christ so that they too might enjoy the peace and happiness that comes through repentance. And as we do this, we will be fulfilling a condition of our repentance. The Lord commanded a few of the early missionaries of the restored Church to continue bearing their testimonies, saying, "I will forgive you of your sins with this commandment—that you remain steadfast . . . in bearing testimony to all the world of those things which are communicated unto you" (D&C 84:61).

The sons of Mosiah, after receiving forgiveness of their sins, were anxious and determined to teach the gospel to the Lamanites. They had been "the very vilest of sinners" and understood the consequences of sin, for they had "suffered much anguish of soul because of their iniquities . . . and fear[ed] that they should be cast off forever" (Mosiah 28:4). They could not rest thinking others would suffer or be denied eternal life:

> They were desirous that salvation should be declared to every creature, for they could not bear that any human soul should perish; yea, even the very thoughts that any soul should endure endless torment did cause them to quake and tremble. (Mosiah 28:3)

Alma the Younger, who had tried to destroy the Church of God along with the sons of Mosiah, unfailingly preached the gospel after his conversion and repentance. He said,

> I have labored without ceasing, that I might bring souls unto repentance; that I might bring them to taste of the exceeding joy of which I did taste; that they might also be born of God, and be filled with the Holy Ghost. (Alma 36:24)

After we receive the Lord's forgiveness and mercy, we will not only desire to share the gospel but also have greater charity and an increased desire to serve others:

> Fulfilling the commandments bringeth remission of sins; and the remission of sins bringeth meekness, and lowliness of heart; and because of meekness and lowliness of heart cometh the visitation of the Holy Ghost, which Comforter filleth with hope and perfect love. (Moroni 8:25–26)

ENDURE TO THE END

Our desires to obey and to share the gospel are the beginning of a life of discipleship. But to be eligible for eternal life, we must continue to do all we can to keep the commandments—we must endure to the end.

Enduring to the end means we are actively engaged in keeping our covenants, serving "God with all diligence day and night" (3 Nephi 5:3), and trying to become more like our Father in Heaven and Jesus Christ. Enduring to the end is overcoming life's trials and trials of our faith.

Through our baptism and confirmation, we "entered in by the gate" and stepped on the "strait and narrow path which leads to eternal life" (2 Nephi 31:18). To return to God's presence, of course, we need to stay on the path (or get back on if we strayed off) and keep moving forward with faith and obedience. Nephi taught,

> After ye have gotten into this strait and narrow path, I would ask if all is done? Behold, I say unto you, Nay. . . . Ye must press forward with a steadfastness in Christ, having a perfect brightness of hope, and a love of God and of all men. Wherefore, if ye shall press forward, feasting upon the word of Christ, and endure to the end, behold, thus saith the Father: Ye shall have eternal life. (2 Nephi 31:19–20)

President Heber J. Grant, who was sick for many months before he passed away, offered this prayer a few weeks prior to his death: "O God, bless me that I shall . . . keep faithful to the end!"[1] An elderly stake patriarch had a similar desire in an anecdote told by Elder M. Russell Ballard:

Shortly after returning from my first mission, I heard our faithful stake patriarch bear his testimony in our ward fast and testimony meeting. He was just over ninety years of age; he said, "I pray every night that God will see me safely dead with my testimony burning brightly." Seeking to comfort this righteous patriarch, I said to him, "Patriarch, I know of no one more prepared than you are." He responded, "My boy, no one is safe until he has endured to the very end of his life."[2]

Enduring to the end is being able to say, as Paul wrote to Timothy, "I have fought a good fight, I have finished my course, I have kept the faith" (2 Timothy 4:7).

ABIDE IN MY LOVE

If we have stumbled in our determination to endure to the end, our transgressions can lead us to feel distant from or unloved by God. The Lord loves us even if we have not kept His commandments, but our sins "have hid his face" (Isaiah 59:2) from us and we are "veiled . . . with darkness" (Moses 7:26). Jesus taught, "If ye keep my commandments, ye shall abide in my love" (John 15:10). But He also declared, "If you keep not my commandments, the love of the Father shall not continue with you" (D&C 95:12).

As we fulfill the conditions of our repentance—as our hearts become softer and our faith and obedience increase—the Spirit begins to return, and we begin to feel a greater measure of the Lord's love for us. When we complete our repentance and are "faithful and diligent in keeping the commandments," we are encircled again "in the arms of [God's] love" (D&C 6:20).

FAVORED OF GOD

The Lord loves His children (see 1 Nephi 11:17) and "is no respecter of persons" (Acts 10:34), yet "he that is righteous is favored of God" (1 Nephi 17:35). Our Father in Heaven causes the sun to rise and the rain to fall on everyone (see Matthew 5:45), but obedience to His commandments enables us to receive additional and specific blessings related to each commandment we obey. The Lord declared, "I . . . am bound when ye do what I say; but when ye do not what I say, ye have no promise" (D&C 82:10). He is not only bound to bless us for our obedience but also enjoys blessing us. He said, "I, the Lord, . . . delight to honor those who serve me in righteousness and in truth unto the end" (D&C 76:5). He also stated, "I delight to bless with the greatest of all blessings, [those] that hear me" (D&C 41:1).

While God rejoices over the righteous, He mourns for His disobedient children. Enoch saw the Lord weep for those who were to be destroyed in the Flood and asked, "How is it thou canst weep?" (Moses 7:31). God replied, "They are the workmanship of mine own hands, and . . . misery shall be their doom; . . . wherefore should not the heavens weep, seeing these shall suffer?" (Moses 7:32, 37).

Our Father in Heaven is saddened beyond our comprehension when we knowingly choose to disobey His commandments or when we choose that "Satan shall be [our] father" (Moses 7:37). But He cannot allow mercy to rob justice if we do not repent (see Alma 42:25), for "there is a law given, and a punishment affixed, and . . . justice claimeth the creature and executeth the law, and the law inflicteth the punishment" (Alma 42:22).

Mormon concisely summarized the disparity between the eternal rewards of the righteous and the wicked when he wrote, "How great the inequality of man is because of sin and transgression" (Alma 28:13). Satan constantly seeks our misery and destruction. But if we keep the commandments, the Lord's promises will be fulfilled, and we will be "raised to dwell at the right hand of God, in a state of never-ending happiness" (Alma 28:12).

NOTES

1. Heber J. Grant, quoted by John Longden, in Conference Report, October 1958, 70.
2. M. Russell Ballard, "The Greater Priesthood: Giving a Lifetime of Service in the Kingdom," *Ensign*, September 1992, 73.

EXTENDING FORGIVENESS: *I* DID FRANKLY *Forgive* THEM

*T*HERE IS, PERHAPS, no greater Christlike gift we can give to others than to sincerely and without reservation forgive them their trespasses against us. The willingness and the ability to forgive is an essential element of charity. Without "the pure love of Christ" (Moroni 7:47), we "forgive not, having not compassion" (D&C 64:13).

"A man filled with the love of God," wrote Joseph Smith, "is . . . anxious to bless the whole human race."[1] When you have charity, you love not only your friends but also your enemies. You "bless them that curse you, do good to them that hate you, and pray for them which despitefully use you" (Matthew 5:44).

We cannot possess the pure love of Christ when our souls are filled with anger, when we seek revenge, or when we find happiness in another person's failure or misfortune. Hatred, bitterness, resentment, retaliation, grudges, and all other similar feelings and actions are the exact opposite to charity and forgiveness.

Charity is "not easily provoked" (Moroni 7:45) and does not render "evil for evil, or railing for railing" (1 Peter 3:9). But charity "thinketh no evil" and "beareth all things" (Moroni 7:45). Charity motivates us to be "kind one to another, tenderhearted, forgiving one another, even as God for Christ's sake hath forgiven you" (Ephesians 4:32).

IF YE FORGIVE NOT

"Except [we] have charity," wrote Moroni, "[we] can in nowise be saved in the kingdom of God" (Moroni 10:21). Nor can we be saved in celestial glory without forgiving others, for it is a condition of our repentance. We are denied the very forgiveness and remission of our sins we need for our salvation if we do not forgive those who have sinned against us. The Lord said, "If ye forgive not men their trespasses, neither will your Father forgive your trespasses" (Matthew 6:15).

How can we plead for mercy and forgiveness from the Lord and not extend the same to others? How can we believe the Atonement of Jesus Christ is effective in our lives but not in the life of someone else?

King Benjamin taught that if we want to retain a remission of our sins, we "should impart of [our] substance . . . both spiritually and temporally" (Mosiah 4:26) to those in need. We can give of our spiritual substance when we forgive others. If, in King Benjamin's counsel to share our earthly goods with the poor, we replace his terms for temporal substance (such as food and riches) with the word *forgiveness*, his instruction becomes a moving admonition to forgive others:

> Are we not all beggars? Do we not all depend upon the same Being, even God, for [forgiveness]? And behold, even at this time, ye have been calling on his name, and begging for a remission of your sins. And has he suffered that ye have begged in vain? Nay; he has poured out his Spirit upon you, and has caused that your hearts should be filled with joy. . . . O then, how ye ought to impart [forgiveness] one to another. (Mosiah 4:19–21)

Jesus emphasized our obligation to forgive one another in the parable of the unmerciful servant:

> Therefore is the kingdom of heaven likened unto a certain king, which would take account of his servants.
>
> And when he had begun to reckon, one was brought unto him, which owed him ten thousand talents. But forasmuch as he had not to pay, his lord commanded him to be sold, and his wife, and children, and all that he had, and payment to be made.
>
> The servant therefore fell down, and worshipped him, saying, Lord, have patience with me, and I will pay thee all. Then the lord

of that servant was moved with compassion, and loosed him, and forgave him the debt.

But the same servant went out, and found one of his fellow-servants, which owed him an hundred pence: and he laid hands on him, and took him by the throat, saying, Pay me that thou owest. And his fellowservant fell down at his feet, and besought him, saying, Have patience with me, and I will pay thee all. And he would not: but went and cast him into prison, till he should pay the debt.

So when his fellowservants saw what was done, they were very sorry, and came and told unto their lord all that was done.

Then his lord, after that he had called him, said unto him, O thou wicked servant, I forgave thee all that debt, because thou desiredst me: Shouldest not thou also have had compassion on thy fellowservant, even as I had pity on thee?

And his lord was wroth, and delivered him to the tormentors, till he should pay all that was due unto him. So likewise shall my heavenly Father do also unto you, if ye from your hearts forgive not every one his brother their trespasses. (Matthew 18:23–35)

We are indebted to our King, our Savior Jesus Christ, for a substantial sum—indeed, for all we have, all we are, and, through His infinite Atonement, all we ever will be. We are justly condemned, as unmerciful servants, if we do not forgive our fellow servants who owe us but relatively little. In addition to being condemned, we are also guilty of the greater sin:

Wherefore, I say unto you, that ye ought to forgive one another; for he that forgiveth not his brother his trespasses standeth condemned before the Lord; for there remaineth in him the greater sin.

I, the Lord, will forgive whom I will forgive, but of you it is required to forgive all men. (D&C 64:9–10)

When we deny forgiveness to others, perhaps we are under condemnation because we are, in a feeble and vain attempt, trying to usurp the Lord's plan of salvation with our own plan of destruction. We are condemning a son or daughter of God without authority, without charity, and with limited knowledge and insight. Instead, we should be extending kindness and mercy to all.

When Heber J. Grant was a relatively new member of the Quorum of the Twelve, he told President Taylor he would not consent to the baptism of an excommunicated man (who had pleaded to be readmitted into the Church on multiple occasions). Shortly after his conversation with President Taylor, Elder Grant went to read from the Doctrine and Covenants, and the book, instead of opening at his bookmark, fell open to the page containing the verses quoted above. He quickly changed his mind, closed the book, and said, "If the devil applies for baptism, and claims that he has repented, I will baptize him."[2]

JUDGMENT IS MINE

When we refuse to forgive, we elevate ourselves to the position of a judge over our transgressors. But Christ said, "Leave judgment alone with me, for it is mine" (D&C 82:23). We "judge after the flesh" (John 8:15), but "the Lord looketh on the heart" (1 Samuel 16:7). Therefore, His "judgment is true" (John 8:16).

Sometimes we add the role of enforcement officer to our self-appointed judgeship to extract a payment or enact a penalty. We desire revenge; we want to administer punishment. We want justice, and we are afraid mercy may be too kind. Yet the Lord has said, "Man shall not smite, . . . vengeance is mine also, and I will repay" (Mormon 8:20).

INCREASE OUR FAITH

Peter asked the Lord, "How oft shall my brother sin against me, and I forgive him?" "Until seventy times seven" (Matthew 18:21–22), replied Jesus. His answer, of course, means we are to forgive others every time they repent. We may humbly utter, as did the Apostles, "Increase our faith" (Luke 17:5). Although it may be difficult for us to forgive others, and we may require the Lord's help to do so, we can forgive them—even of the most horrendous sins.

Nephi "did frankly forgive" (1 Nephi 7:21) his brothers of their attempt to leave him bound in the wilderness to be eaten by wild animals. Joseph, who was sold into Egypt, forgave his brothers when they came to Egypt to buy grain. After revealing his identity to them, he said, "Now therefore be not grieved, nor angry with yourselves, that ye sold me hither: for God did send me before you to preserve life" (Genesis 45:5). He rejoiced to be with them again, and "he kissed all his brethren, and wept upon them" (Genesis 45:15).

W. W. Phelps, whose betrayal and false testimony contributed to Joseph Smith's confinement in Liberty Jail, wrote Joseph and requested readmission into the Church:

> I am as the prodigal son. . . . I have seen the folly of my way, and I tremble at the gulf I have passed. . . . I know my situation, you know it, and God knows it, and I want to be saved if my friends will help me. . . . I have done wrong and I am sorry. The beam is in my own eye. . . . I ask forgiveness in the name of Jesus Christ of all the Saints, for I will do right, God helping me. . . . I will make all the satisfaction on every point that Saints or God can require.[3]

Joseph responded with these beautiful, forgiving words:

> Truly our hearts were melted into tenderness and compassion when we ascertained your resolves. . . .
>
> It is true, that we have suffered much in consequence of your behavior—the cup of gall, already full enough for mortals to drink, was indeed filled to overflowing when you turned against us. . . .
>
> Believing your confession to be real, and your repentance genuine, I shall be happy once again to give you the right hand of fellowship, and rejoice over the returning prodigal. . . .
>
> "Come on, dear brother, since the war is past,
> For friends at first, are friends again at last."[4]

FROM YOUR HEARTS FORGIVE

Like every condition of our repentance, we must forgive others with real intent. The Lord said,

> My disciples, in days of old, sought occasion against one another and forgave not one another *in their hearts*; and for this evil they were afflicted and sorely chastened. (D&C 64:8; emphasis added)

We can forgive from our hearts when our hearts are filled with charity. After we have forgiven a transgression committed against us, we never mention the offense again—to the person who committed the sin or to anyone else. We stop replaying the sin in our minds, for the continued rehearsal only serves to preserve our hurt and anger.

There can be no lingering resentment or retention of the smallest fiber of hatred. We turn it over to the Lord, and we leave it alone.

Private offenses are kept private. You should keep an individual's trespass against you, when appropriate, "between him or her and thee alone" (D&C 42:88) so that you are free from the sins of gossip and sowing contention and so that others "may not speak reproachfully" (D&C 42:92) of the person who committed the sin.

You are required of the Lord to forgive without reservation (except as noted in the last section of this chapter). Even if your transgressor does not fulfill any condition of his repentance, you should still forgive him. In fact, instead of waiting for him to come to you, you should approach him, for "if he shall hear thee, thou hast gained thy brother" (Matthew 18:15).

As we extend mercy to others, the Lord will grant us mercy. "Blessed are the merciful," Jesus taught His disciples, "for they shall obtain mercy" (Matthew 5:7). Joseph Smith, expressing his desire to emulate the Lord's mercy, wrote,

> Inasmuch as long-suffering, patience, and mercy have ever characterized the dealings of our heavenly Father towards the humble and penitent, I feel disposed to copy the example, cherish the same principles, and by so doing be a savior of my fellow men.[5]

FORGIVING OTHERS SETS YOU FREE

In a fast and testimony meeting years ago, a member of our ward shared with us how she had become cold and uncaring because she was hurt and unwilling to forgive. As a teenager she had wondered how some people could become so hardhearted, and yet, she said, she had become like them. She continued by saying that she had recently moved into a new home, but she found her feelings of bitterness and pain had followed her there. After reflecting on her situation, she realized that if she wanted to be happy again, it was her heart, not her surroundings, that needed to change. She then bore testimony of the healing power of the Atonement and of the peace she found after forgiving her offender.

Our spiritual progress will be hindered, even reversed, when we refuse to forgive others. With a forgiving heart we can resign our positions of "judge, jury, and executioner" and move forward in more uplifting and productive pursuits. Most important, like the member in the story above, forgiving others will release us from anger, bitterness, and resentment and bring us joy and inner peace.

Corrie ten Boom, a survivor of the Ravensbrück concentration camp in Germany, established a home for Holocaust victims after the end of World War II. She observed firsthand the crippling effects that can occur when we refuse to forgive others:

> Those who were able to forgive their former enemies were able also to return to the outside world and rebuild their lives, no matter what the physical scars. Those who nursed their bitterness remained invalids. It was as simple and as horrible as that.[6]

FORGIVING YOURSELF

While counseling his son Helaman, Alma said, "I had rebelled against my God, and . . . I had not kept his holy commandments" (Alma 36:13). He then explained to Helaman one of the great blessings he received from being forgiven, saying, "I was harrowed up by the memory of my sins no more" (Alma 36:19). Alma could still remember his past sins, but the memory of his sins no longer caused him any pain. Why? Because he had repented and had been forgiven, and he knew he had been forgiven. He had experienced the manifestations of divine forgiveness. He exultantly declared, "What joy, and what marvelous light I did behold; yea, my soul was filled with joy" (Alma 36:20).

After you have completed all the conditions of your repentance and received divine forgiveness, accept the Lord's forgiveness and forgive yourself. President Hugh B. Brown, formerly of the First Presidency, counseled, "[You] should not persist in remembering that which the Lord has said He is willing to forget."[7] Elder Richard G. Scott, addressing those who cannot forgive themselves for serious past sins, said,

> I testify that when a bishop or stake president has confirmed that your repentance is sufficient, know that your obedience has allowed the Atonement of Jesus Christ to satisfy the demands of justice for the laws you have broken. Therefore you are now free. Please

believe it. To continually suffer the distressing effects of sin after adequate repentance, while not intended, is to deny the efficacy of the Savior's Atonement in your behalf.[8]

THOU SHALT NOT FORGIVE HIM

Although we are commanded to forgive, we do not need to ignore, tolerate, or even accept every transgression against us. It is appropriate to "appeal to the civil law for redress of all wrongs and grievances, where personal abuse is inflicted or the right of property or character infringed" (D&C 134:11). Certainly, if we are in imminent physical danger, we should protect and defend ourselves. "We believe," states the declaration on government and laws in the Doctrine and Covenants, "that all men are justified in defending themselves, their friends, and property, . . . from the unlawful assaults . . . of all persons in times of exigency [emergency]" (D&C 134:11).

We forgive "as oft as [our] *enemy repenteth*" (D&C 98:40; emphasis added). But if our adversary does not repent and continues to repeatedly commit the same sin against us, we are justified in withholding our forgiveness. "Thou shalt not forgive him" (D&C 98:44), said the Lord. However, if we "bear it patiently and revile not against [him]" (D&C 98:23), the Lord will bless us abundantly.

NOTES

1. Joseph Smith, *History of the Church of Jesus Christ of Latter-day Saints* (Salt Lake City: The Church of Jesus Christ of Latter-day Saints, 1949), 4:227.
2. Heber J. Grant, in Conference Report, October 1920, 6.
3. Smith, *History of the Church*, 4:141–42.
4. Ibid., 4:163–64.
5. Ibid., 4:163.
6. Corrie ten Boom, "I'm Still Learning to Forgive," Guideposts, November 1972, 4.
7. Hugh B. Brown, quoted by Thomas S. Monson, "Mercy—The Divine Gift," *Ensign*, May 1995, 60.
8. Richard G. Scott, "Peace of Conscience and Peace of Mind," *Ensign*, November 2004, 18.

SEEKING FORGIVENESS: EXCEEDINGLY *Great* JOY

OUR FATHER IN Heaven, knowing "all the thoughts and intents of the heart" (Alma 18:32; see also D&C 6:16), may grant us forgiveness before we have completed all the conditions of our repentance—perhaps even before we have asked Him for forgiveness.[1] Usually, however, the final condition of our repentance is to ask God "in sincerity of heart that he would forgive [us]" (Mosiah 4:10).

Although it may seem obvious, we need to ask forgiveness from Heavenly Father for all our sins. Even when we have sinned against others, and they have forgiven us, we still need to seek divine forgiveness for those transgressions. Similarly, if your Church membership privileges were suspended, you should ask God, before you are received back into full fellowship, for forgiveness for those sins that led to your Church discipline. Others can forgive us and your bishop can restore privileges, but only God can absolve us from our iniquities.

YOUR SINS ARE FORGIVEN YOU

When we have fulfilled all the other conditions of our repentance and our change of heart is complete, we qualify for and can seek God's forgiveness. Our Father in Heaven has promised He will forgive us. He declared, "Whosoever repenteth, and hardeneth not his heart, he shall have claim on mercy through mine Only Begotten Son, unto a remission of his sins" (Alma 12:34).

In our prayers for forgiveness, we plead with God to spare us from the full demands of justice "through the merits, and mercy, and grace of the Holy Messiah" (2 Nephi 2:8) and to free us from sin's current heavy burden (see Matthew 11:28). We seek to be washed clean "through the atoning blood of Jesus Christ" (Helaman 5:9) and to be found worthy to one day "sit down with Abraham, and Isaac, and Jacob, in the kingdom of heaven" (Matthew 8:11). We desire with all our hearts to be forgiven and to receive a remission of our sins. Elder Spencer W. Kimball wrote,

> Sometimes . . . guilt . . . overpowers a person with such a heaviness that when a repentant one looks back and sees the ugliness, the loathsomeness of the transgression, he is almost overwhelmed and wonders, "Can the Lord ever forgive me? Can I ever forgive myself?" But when one reaches the depths of despondency and feels the hopelessness of his position, and when he cries out to God for mercy in helplessness but in faith, there comes a still, small, but penetrating voice whispering to his soul, "Thy sins are forgiven thee."[2]

There is no feeling more sublime, more comforting, or more reassuring than when the Spirit conveys to us the Lord's words of forgiveness: "Behold, your sins are forgiven you; you are clean before me; therefore, lift up your head and rejoice" (D&C 110:5; changed to singular form). What "exceedingly great joy" (Mosiah 4:11) and "peace of conscience" (Mosiah 4:3) we will feel! Our guilt is swept away (see Enos 1:6), and our souls are flooded with "the light of everlasting life" (Alma 19:6).

Alma the Younger, before he was forgiven, was horrified at the thought of being brought before God. He said,

> So great had been my iniquities, that the very thought of coming into the presence of my God did rack my soul with inexpressible horror. Oh, thought I, that I could be banished and become extinct both soul and body, that I might not be brought to stand in the presence of my God, to be judged of my deeds. (Alma 36:14–15)

But after he was forgiven, he yearned to be in God's presence:

> Yea, methought I saw . . . God sitting upon his throne, surrounded with numberless concourses of angels, in the attitude of singing and praising their God; yea, and my soul did long to be there. (Alma 36:22)

What a difference being cleansed of sin makes! We are purged of all our feelings of unworthiness and worthlessness, for we are now worthy and accepted of the Lord. We have been healed by the Master Physician and made spiritually whole. He removed our "stony heart" and gave us each "a new heart . . . and a new spirit" (Ezekiel 36:26). We have "become new creatures" (Mosiah 27:26). We are no longer who we once were nor are we defined by our old sins. We have returned to righteousness and become more like our Savior.

We can now look forward to "that glorious day when justice shall be administered unto the righteous, even the day of judgment" (2 Nephi 9:46), for "none of [our] sins . . . shall be mentioned unto [us]" (Ezekiel 33:16). The Lord will "remember them no more" (D&C 58:42).

ON CONDITIONS OF REPENTANCE

Nephi taught "that it is by grace that we are saved, after all we can do" (2 Nephi 25:23). While teaching the same principle, Alma the Younger referred his listeners to the example of his father and the people who were baptized at the waters of Mormon and asked, "On what conditions are they saved? Yea, what grounds had they to hope for salvation? What is the cause of their being loosed from . . . the chains of hell?" (Alma 5:10). Answering his own questions, he said, "A mighty change was . . . wrought in their hearts, and . . . they were faithful until the end" (Alma 5:13).

You have become clean through your repentance—your mighty change of heart—and through the redeeming power of Jesus Christ. The Lord rejoices that you have returned to Him, for you are of great worth and precious in His sight (see D&C 18:10; Isaiah 43:4). He declared, "How great is [my] joy in the soul that repenteth!" (D&C 18:13).

In 1919, Elder Melvin J. Ballard, a member of the Quorum of the Twelve, spoke of a dream he had in which he met the Savior and felt of His love and approval:

> He took me into his arms and kissed me, pressed me to his bosom, and blessed me, until the marrow of my bones seemed to melt! . . . To have his love, his affection, and his blessing was such that if I ever can receive that of which I had but a foretaste, I would give all that I am, all that I ever hope to be, to feel what I then felt![3]

Jesus Christ, the Redeemer of the world, loves you. He came to save you—to save us all (see 1 Timothy 1:15). He suffered "the pain of all men . . . that he might bring all men unto him, *on conditions of repentance*" (D&C 18:11–12; emphasis added).

NOTES

1. Alma the Younger, who was tormented by his many transgressions for three days, said, "Never, until I did cry out unto the Lord Jesus Christ for mercy, did I receive a remission of my sins" (Alma 38:8). Even though he repented with a complete change of heart and was forgiven (see Mosiah 27:24), Alma then completed his repentance by making restitution and confessing his sins to King Mosiah's people (see Mosiah 27:35). Lyman Sherman, on the other hand, was forgiven of his sins without apparently asking for forgiveness. He followed a prompting to seek a revelation through Joseph Smith, and the Lord told him, "Your sins are forgiven you, because you have obeyed my voice in coming up hither this morning to receive counsel of him whom I have appointed" (D&C 108:1).

2. Spencer W. Kimball, *The Miracle of Forgiveness* (Salt Lake City: Bookcraft, 1969), 344.

3. Melvin J. Ballard, "The Sacramental Covenant," *Improvement Era*, October 1919, 1032.

BIBLIOGRAPHY

Ballard, M. Russell. "The Greater Priesthood: Giving a Lifetime of Service in the Kingdom." *Ensign*, September 1992.

Ballard, Melvin J. "The Sacramental Covenant." *Improvement Era*, October 1919.

Bednar, David A. "And Nothing Shall Offend Them." *Ensign*, November 2006.

Benson, Ezra Taft. "Beware of Pride." *Ensign*, May 1989.

——. "Cleansing the Inner Vessel." *Ensign*, May 1986.

——. "Counsel to the Saints." *Ensign*, May 1984.

——. "A Mighty Change of Heart." *Ensign*, October 1989.

Brown, Hugh B., quoted by Thomas S. Monson. "Mercy—The Divine Gift." *Ensign*, May 1995.

Burton, Theodore M. "The Meaning of Repentance." *Ensign*, August 1988.

Clark, J. Reuben, Jr. Conference Report, April 1950.

Cowdery, Oliver. *Latter Day Saints' Messenger and Advocate*, February 1835.

Davidson, Karen Lynn, David J. Whittaker, Mark Ashurst-McGee, and Richard L. Jensen, eds. *Histories, Volume 1: Joseph Smith Histories, 1832–1844*. Vol. 1 of the Histories series of *The Joseph Smith Papers,* edited by Dean C. Jessee, Ronald K. Esplin, and Richard Lyman Bushman. Salt Lake City: Church Historian's Press, 2012.

Featherstone, Vaughn J. "'Forgive Them, I Pray Thee.'" *Ensign*, November 1980.

——. *A Generation of Excellence: A Guide for Parents and Youth Leaders.* Salt Lake City: Bookcraft, 1975.

The First Presidency and Council of the Twelve Apostles. "The Family: A Proclamation to the World." *Ensign*, November 1995.

Grant, Heber J. Conference Report, October 1920.

——, quoted by John Longden. Conference Report, October 1958.

Hanks, Marion D. "He Means Me." *Ensign*, May 1979.

BIBLIOGRAPHY

Journal of Discourses. 26 vols. London: Latter-day Saints' Book Depot, 1854–1886.

Kimball, Heber C. "Synopsis of the History of Heber Chase Kimball." *The Deseret News*, April 21, 1858.

Kimball, Spencer W. Conference Report, October 1949.

——. *The Miracle of Forgiveness*. Salt Lake City: Bookcraft, 1969.

"A Letter from a Young Person." *Calgary Community Conferencing Newsletter*, October 2001.

Maxwell, Neal A. "Repentance." *Ensign*, November 1991.

Monson, Thomas S. "As We Meet Together Again." *Ensign*, November 2010.

Oaks, Dallin H. " 'Faith in the Lord Jesus Christ.' " *Ensign*, May 1994.

——. "Sin and Suffering." *Ensign*, July 1992.

——. "Sins and Mistakes." *Ensign*, October 1996.

Packer, Boyd K. *The Holy Temple*. Salt Lake City: Bookcraft, 1980.

Pope, Alexander. *An Essay on Man. In Epistles to a Friend. Epistle II.* London: Printed for J. Wilford, 1733.

Robinson, Stephen E. *Believing Christ: The Parable of the Bicycle and Other Good News*. Salt Lake City: Deseret Book, 1992.

Romney, Marion G. Conference Report, October 1955.

Rudd, Glen L. "Keeping the Gospel Simple." *Ensign*, January 1989, and *Tambuli*, March 1990.

Scott, Richard G. "Peace of Conscience and Peace of Mind." *Ensign*, November 2004.

Smith, Joseph. *History of The Church of Jesus Christ of Latter-day Saints*. 7 vols. Salt Lake City: The Church of Jesus Christ of Latter-day Saints, 1932–1951.

——. *Lectures on Faith*. Salt Lake City: Deseret Book, 1985.

Smith, Joseph F. *Gospel Doctrine*. Salt Lake City: Deseret Book, 1986.

Smith, Joseph Fielding. Conference Report, April 1969.

Smith, Lucy Mack. *The Revised and Enhanced History of Joseph Smith By His Mother*. Edited by Scot Facer Proctor and Maurine Jensen Proctor. Salt Lake City: Bookcraft, 1996.

Talmage, James E. *Jesus The Christ*. Salt Lake City: The Church of Jesus Christ of Latter-day Saints, 1981.

ten Boom, Corrie. "I'm Still Learning to Forgive." *Guideposts*, November 1972.

Whittier, John G. *Maud Muller*. Boston: Ticknor and Fields, 1867.

SCRIPTURE INDEX

Scripture Index

Matthew

3:17	58n1
4:20	46
5:7	124
5:21–22	73
5:27–28	73
5:28	23
5:44	119
5:45	117
5:48	5
6:14 (JST)	78
6:15	120
8:11	128
11:28	94, 128
18:15	124
18:21–22	122
18:23–35	121
19:16	77
19:20–22	77
21:28–31	102
23:34	70
25:1–13	42
25:23	26

Luke

7:37–48	64
7:50	64
12:47–48	20
13:4–5	72
15:32	18
17:5	122
19:5–9	99
22:31–32	35

John

3:16	13
4:16–19	54
5:39	1
8:9	68

8:11	112
8:15	122
8:16	122
8:24	60
8:44	34
15:10	117

Acts

2:37–38	70
5:1–11	93
10:34	117
17:30	44

Romans

3:23	6
5:12	1, 14
6:1–2	105
10:1	77
10:3	77
13:12	106
14:10–12	94

1 Corinthians

2:14	28
10:13	18
15:22	14

2 Corinthians

7:9–10	81
7:10	83, 92

Galatians

5:22	27

Ephesians

4:32	119

1 Timothy

1:15	130
4:2	68

2 Timothy

4:7	117

SCRIPTURE INDEX

SCRIPTURE INDEX

SUBJECT INDEX

A

Abortion, 23

Adam: Fall of, 5–6, 14, 63, 114; role in premortal life, 34

Addiction, 109

Adultery, 20, 23, 73, 108–09

Adversities, see Trials

Agency: a gift from God, 33; loss of, 29; necessary for progression, 40; necessary for repentance, 111; no sin without, 52; Satan seeks to destroy man's, 33; through knowledge, 52; through temptations, 35

Anger, 73, 109–10

Atonement, see Jesus Christ, Atonement of

B

Ballard, M. Russell, story of his stake patriarch who wants to endure to the end, 116–17

Ballard, Melvin J., dreams of seeing the Savior, 129–30

Bednar, David A., visits offended members, 53–54

Benson, Ezra Taft: on desire for eternal family, 26; on pride, 50; on reformation of behavior, 60; on sexual sin, 22

Bishop (see also Confession, to the bishop): accepting counsel from, 53, 70; cannot

absolve sins, 127; clearance from, 125; responsibilities of, 91–92; role of, 92

Blessings: loss of, 29, 43; predicated on obedience, 28–29, 117

Brown, Hugh B., on forgiving yourself, 125

Burton, Theodore M., on repentance, 8

C

Celestial kingdom, 25, 38, 39

Charity, 9, 119–20

Chastening, 71–72, 86

Chastity, 22–23, 56, 61, 102, 108, 111, 113–14

Church discipline, 28, 91–92, 127

Church membership, privileges of, 30n3

Clark, J. Reuben, on confessing sins, 92

Confession: delayed, 94–96; no forgiveness without, 97; of all sins, 89, 94; partial, 54–55, 93–94; to others, 90; to the bishop, 55, 91–92, 95–97; to the Lord, 90; voluntary, 92

Conscience, 39, 68, 128

Counsel, accepting, 53, 70

Counseling, professional, 110

Covenants, 19, 20, 108, 113

man, 122; man counsels an unhappy wife, 69; man loses blessings while he is sinning, 29; man loses the energy to sin, 111; man tries to overcome his quick temper, 109–10; Martin Harris loses the first 116 pages of the Book of Mormon, 83–84; Matt prepares for the future, 45; Melvin J. Ballard dreams of seeing the Savior, 129–30; stake patriarch wants to endure to the end, 116–17; Syd forsakes smoking, 106–07; two women react differently to their pregnancies, 22; Vaughn J. Featherstone interviews a young adult for a mission, 55–57; W. W. Phelps asks forgiveness, 123; woman forgives her offender, 124; young man writes a letter of apology, 100–01

*D*AVID P. FISLER has nearly twenty years of local leadership experience in The Church of Jesus Christ of Latter-day Saints as a high councilor, counselor in multiple bishoprics and in a branch presidency, bishop, and young single adult branch president. As a young man, he served as a full-time missionary in the Mexico Hermosillo Mission.

He and his wife, Joan, are the parents of four children and live in San Diego, California.